A Preface to
Psychology

D1482121

A Preface to Psychology

Cameron Fincher

Georgia State College

HARPER & ROW, Publishers
New York, Evanston, and London

FOR CARL AND CLARICE

Contents

Preface

This brief book has been written for those who would take the study of psychology seriously. Its avowed purpose is to help establish a receptive attitude to the pursuit of psychology as an empirical science and to provide a bridge for understanding human behavior in terms of systematic inquiry. Operationally, the book is a brief overview of the philosophical characteristics of science, the historical development of psychology as a science of behavior, and the methods by which behavior can be studied.

The author's biases will be obvious. He believes that no one can properly appreciate psychology without some knowledge of science, a familiarity with the historical antecedents of contemporary psychology, and a thorough understanding of psychological methods of investigation. He further believes that new acquaintances should be introduced as quickly as possible to the conceptual tools of psychology and to the procedures followed in gaining knowledge of human behavior. There is a firm insistence that empirical facts and findings are the substance of psychology and that an understanding of the facts must be based on an understanding of the methods by which they are acquired.

Although intended as supplementary reading in introductory psychology courses, the book should serve instructional purposes in other courses. Other behavioral scientists may find something of value within these pages, and it is not inconceivable that the general public might. In addition, the author has frequently found that advanced psychology students need periodic reinforcement as to the purposes and functions of psychology as a natural science.

The contents of this book have been improved considerably by the suggestions and criticisms of Dr. Robert B. Freeman, Jr.; his careful reading of the manuscript saved the author from errors of both fact and interpretation. Acknowledgments are also due Miss Irma Daniels for preparing the manuscript, Mrs. Polly

Simpson for proofing chores and assistance with the index, and Thomas F. McDonald for providing the spare moments in which the book was written.

CAMERON FINCHER

Atlanta, Georgia
March, 1964

A Preface to
Psychology

Psychology and
Common Sense　　**1**

A theory of human behavior is implicit in all our social, political, economic, and religious activities. As a theory, it is often incomplete, usually naïve, and seldom consistent. Yet, underlying all our actions and conduct is a system of beliefs, opinions, and attitudes concerning what human nature is, what it can be, and what it ought to be.

What we believe human nature to be influences both how we act and what we accomplish. It affects the relations we establish with others, the expectations we have of them, and the manner in which we deal with them; it has great bearing on how we raise our children, what we strive to teach them, and the plans we make for their future. It touches and alters the way we conduct business, produce goods and services, distribute rights and privileges, enact and enforce laws, dispense justice, and worship. No area of human endeavor is unaffected by our knowledge and understanding of human behavior.

For the most part, our theory of human behavior is given to us readymade, and it may run the course of our lives without being brought to serious question. It is a function of our cultural heritage and it reflects our socioeconomic background, our home and community environment, our educational attainments, and our occupational achievements. If someone is impudent enough to question our beliefs and opinions concerning human nature, most of us are forced to appeal to the authority of common sense. To each of us it is only natural that we should believe as we do, and we do not hesitate to assert that what we believe is common sense.

Our appeal to common sense is delusive. Common sense will not serve as an adequate authority because common sense is seldom what we suppose it to be. If all of us were as amply endowed with common sense as we suppose, we would all be excellent mathematicians—because mathematics is exactly the kind of clear-cut, irrefutable logic that we suppose common sense to be. Much to the contrary, we find that common sense is a not-so-common characteristic of our society, and we no longer can appeal to absolute, fixed notions of human behavior.

Magic, Mythology, and Metaphysics

Many of our beliefs and opinions concerning human nature have their origin in folklore and superstition, and some have an unbroken history from darkest antiquity. Modern science has altered radically the perspective with which we must view human nature, but the tenacity with which we cling to certain fallacies, misconceptions, and prejudices is incredible.

There is great irony in the fact that one of civilized man's first systematic efforts to explain his own behavior began with the most distant events in the universe. The ancient Egyptians and Babylonians observed the movement of celestial spheres and concluded that the regularity of human behavior could be accounted for by the regularity of the stars. Some unknown genius hypothesized that the position of the stars at the time of an individual's birth determined the course of his life, and astrology has been a booming business ever since.

Despite the absurdity of astrology as an explanation of human behavior, it was an improvement over preceding explanations and a beginning of behavioral science as we know it. Primitive man had seen his own behavior as subject to the caprice of animistic forces. He lived in a world of evil spirits, and his only protection was to devise magical rites to ward off those that were harmful and to attract those that were beneficial. His principles of magic were simple and direct. One event caused another if they were similar in appearance, or one event caused another because they were near each other in space or time. Armed with this knowledge of the hostile forces surrounding him, primitive man tried to control them through imitative action. An enemy could be destroyed by constructing and then destroying a likeness of him; the enemy could be controlled by gaining possession of his hair, eyebrows, fingernails, or some other part of his body. Even possession of an enemy's name gave one great power over him.

Sympathetic magic was not, needless to say, an adequate explanation of man's behavior, but it implied a rigorous determinism. If one's magical rites did not produce the desired effect, it was only because the enemy's magic was more potent. The solution was to seek a more powerful form of magic, and so primitive man was engaged in an arms race of incantations, rites, ceremonies, amulets, and talismans.

In mythology the forces of nature were stripped of much of their animism and cast in an anthropomorphic form. This, no doubt, was more appealing to man's vanity, but it resulted in a reduction of his control over nature. The deities and celestial beings of mythology were as fickle and capricious as the animistic spirits they replaced, but man's rites and ceremonies could no longer control—they could only propitiate. Once again at the mercy of supernatural forces, man could escape fate only through intervention of an equally potent but more sympathetic deity. The notion of fate implied in mythological explanations was essentially pessimistic and suggested that man himself could do little to avoid what the future held in store.

Fate was also an essential component of astrology. Yet, astrology was an improvement over animism and mythology because it recognized an orderliness and a regularity to man's behavior. This meant that he was no longer subject to the whims of animistic forces or capricious deities, and he could quietly resign himself to fate without worrying about magical methods of combat. It was man's first effort at a naturalistic explanation of his behavior. It also gave one grounds for optimism—if one were born under the right sign.

Regardless of its advantages over animism and mythology, astrology, as a theory of behavior, is fallacious. The movement of the stars tells us nothing about the movement of men. In devising his elaborate system of astrological non-sense, civilized man made the same mistake that his primitive ancestor did. He assumed a causal relationship between celestial spheres and human behavior because both displayed an orderly progression in time. His reasoning was still subject to the first law of sympathetic magic, the principle of similarity. Civilized man is still subject to the same error of logic but in a more subtle fashion. We no longer believe in the principle of causation through similarity but a tendency to "reason by analogy" is still prevalent in much of our thinking about human conduct.

Both animistic and mythological interpretations of human behavior are metaphysical in that they go beyond the physical world of man to seek a cause for his behavior in nonphysical events and entities. In more recent history, however, metaphysical explanations of man's behavior have not invoked animistic spirits and mythological deities as much as they have involved a dualism of mind and matter.

The mind-body problem is one of the oldest snarls in philosophy. Plato's distinction between natural phenomena and their true essence has remained a source of confusion for 2400 years, and his creation of a world of mind as opposed to a world of matter may be regarded as his most dubious contribution to western civilization. In one form or another, his notion of the human body as a physical entity existing in space and the mind as a nonmaterial entity coexisting with the body has plagued everyone who seeks to explain the actions and conduct of man. According to Platonic idealism, the body is subject to the laws of nature and it is impermanent; the mind does not operate according to known laws of nature and its existence does not terminate with the body. The mind thinks, feels, and wills; the body heeds, responds, and obeys.

The classical distinction between mind and body has disrupted attempts to explain human behavior in two ways. First, it has required an explanation of behavior, which is observable, in terms of events and processes which are unobservable and intangible. Too often, this takes the form of "an invisible ghost who commands and directs body movements and actions." The result has often been that man has succeeded only in attributing to mind the properties and characteristics of animism and mythology.

The second way in which the mind-body distinction disturbs our attempts to understand human behavior is seen in our many futile efforts to determine mental traits and characteristics from man's physical features. This may be regarded as an effort to establish two-way traffic over a bridge that we imagine to be built over Plato's chasm. Not only does man seek to explain his overt behavior in terms of mind, but he has devised elaborate means of determining mind from observable features of the body. The quest, of course, is for a simple, easy key which will give us access to the inner world of personality and character.

Perhaps the earliest attempt to explain behavior in terms of physical features is Hippocrates' classification of temperament types by body humors. Translating the four elements of the cosmos, earth, air, fire, and water, into bodily humors of blood, yellow bile, black bile, and phlegm, Hippocrates ascribed a different type of temperament to an excess of the relevant humor. Persons who were sanguine (quick, gay, unstable) were believed to have an excess of blood; those who were choleric (quick to anger) had an excess of yellow bile; those who were melancholic (depressed, pessimistic) had an excess of black bile; and those who were phlegmatic (slow, unexcitable) had excessive phlegm.

Similar efforts to link characteristics of mind with physical features are seen in the many systems of physiognomy or characterology that have been devised in more recent years. They all have one thing in common; they are all efforts to gain easy access to the world of mind by means of a physical key. Phrenology in the nineteenth century sought to diagnose personality and character traits by "reading the bumps" on an individual's head; palmistry seeks access by reading the lines in the palm of the hand; and somatypists try to ascertain personality and temperament by classification of body type.

Vestiges of Prescientific Thought

Much of man's prescientific effort to explain human behavior is still common currency in contemporary thought and discussion. Despite countless refutations of his claims, the astrologist still survives. His books may be bought at almost any magazine stand and his advice may be sought in almost any daily newspaper. Publishers and editors are quick to claim that they publish horoscopes for entertainment purposes only, but the advent of the space age has given astrology an unbelievable "respectability" and it is more lucrative today than it has ever been.

Astrology is but one of many pseudosciences explaining human behavior to the general public. There are numerous other self-styled experts who, for an appropriate fee, diagnose behavioral problems and prescribe infallible cures, predict the future and assure fame or fortune, transmit special powers of attraction and charm, advise on personal matters such as love and marriage, and assist in regaining lost abilities, lost friends, and lost possessions. The claims of such experts on human behavior are preposterous, but only the naïve would contend that no one takes these experts seriously. If we may judge from the obvious commercial success of many charlatans, we must conclude that someone very definitely takes them seriously. But pseudoscientific notions of behavior are not sustained solely by those who have an economic motive. The mystical and the occult have an amazingly strong appeal, even among educated people, and where the promise of mystery, magic, and intrigue is present, it is not difficult to find someone who will believe. All of us harbor foolish suppositions about human nature and most of us are susceptible to a childlike desire to believe in the occult, the magical, and the mysterious. Superstition and ignorance continue to clutter our thinking where others are concerned; we are still susceptible to promises of a quick index to personality and temperament.

Adherents to the various schemes of characterology are often found among intelligent, educated people. Characterology is closely related to our well-known propensity for thinking in terms of stereotypes; it reflects the tenacious belief that people can be classified into a few simple, distinctive types and that we are able to classify them by physical appearance. The most widely known system of this kind specifies that tall, skinny people are shy, reserved, and withdrawn, while short, fat people are happy, jolly, and friendly.

In much the same vein, many people will readily concede that blondes are frivolous, scatterbrained, dizzy, and fickle, whereas brunettes are reliable, stable, and passionate. If hair color doesn't provide a suitable key to the individual's personality and character, then most of us feel competent to judge from his face; it is well known that a high brow denotes intelligence, small ears indicate stinginess, and the person who does not look you in the eye obviously isn't telling the truth. Novelists still rely heavily on a description of facial features to convey the "inner qualities" of their characters, and we seldom encounter a hero with a weak chin.

Rather than being a system of axiomatic truth and irrefutable logic, common sense, where human behavior is concerned, is still too much a bagatelle of animism, mythology, and metaphysics.

A Science of Behavior

Human nature and conduct may be interpreted from many points of views. Philosophers, theologians, poets, and artists have supplied conceptions of man's behavior, and the varieties of permissible interpretations are numerous. The notion that the methods of natural science could be applied to the study of man's behavior is a recent one, however, and psychologists must be regarded as late starters in the game.

As a natural scientist, the psychologist believes that human behavior can be studied by methods and procedures similar to those found successful in the physical and biological sciences. The psychologist does not deny the value of literary, artistic, philosophical, and theological interpretations of human nature, but he is skeptical of their adequacy as explanations of behavior. The psychologist believes that a scientific explanation of behavior should involve no assumptions of supernatural agencies. He rejects speculation as a method of acquiring knowledge about behavior and appeals directly to experience—the observation of actual behavior. The psychologist cannot accept uncritically the conclusions of custom and tradition, especially in the form of folklore and superstition; he must develop a willingness to proceed from the simple to the complex; and he must be willing to tolerate uncertainty in his quest for an understanding of behavior. In brief, the psychologist must investigate the complexities of behavior according to the "rules of the game" set forth by natural science.

In his scientific study of human behavior, the psychologist is not alone. Anthropologists, sociologists, economists, and political scientists also study human behavior, and each applies his own methods and techniques to the area of behavior in which he is interested. There is reason to believe, however, that the psychologist studies behavior more intensively than any other scientist. To the psychologist behavior is an inclusive phenomenon; more than the mere overt movements of man, behavior includes all observable activities of a living organism functioning as a unit.

In order to understand how psychologists study behavior, we shall digress somewhat in the following chapter for a discussion of what science is. After identifying the distinctive characteristics of science as a method of inquiry, we shall consider the historical development of psychology as a science. Although psychology must claim a short history, an appreciation of its rapid and vigorous development is essential to an understanding of its current status and contributions. In Chapter 4 we shall return to the discussion of a science of behavior and its methods of investigation.

Some
Characteristics
of Science 2

Although the twentieth century is less than two-thirds past, it is safe to predict that it will be remembered as an age of science. We may seriously question whether future historians will be enthralled with our contributions in art, literature, music, philosophy, and theology, but we may rest assured that they will not ignore the innovations of twentieth-century science.

Only science can claim continuous progress from the seventeenth century, an age of vigorous exploration and discovery. Continuity may be traced in our artistic, literary, musical, and philosophical endeavors, but we would do well not to stress inevitable progress as their most salient feature. Many critics of contemporary society have suggested that not only have we failed to progress in these areas but we have actually suffered decline.

No such critics of science may be found. There are many who have not always agreed with the turns taken by science and there are others who are not overly enthused about prospects for the future, but all will agree that the strides taken by science within the past sixty years have been fantastic. Science and its alter ego, technology, have modified every phase and aspect of man's existence. Even our superstitions have taken on scientific trappings in order to be more palatable to us.

Science's progress has not been inexorable, however. Scientists have made false starts, fumbled opportunities, and frequently been distracted. But they have been fighting a constant rear guard action against ignorance and supersition, and progress has been continuous—a tribute, no doubt, to the versatility of scientists.

Science, despite its impact on our lives, is not easy to define. Like ethics, it may be defined in terms of its intentions, its actions, and its consequences, but none of these really conveys a proper appreciation of science as a form of intellectual inquiry. Attempts to define science have a way of skirting its many features and eventually settling down to a discussion of scientific methods. Perhaps we can best define science here by identifying its most distinctive characteristics.

Science is rational; it employs reason. A rationalist may be defined as a man who believes some good can come out of deductive logic. For the sake of argument, he accepts as true certain statements and then reasons from the general to the particular. Aristotle set forth the laws of deductive logic over two thousand years ago, and in western civilization they have never been repealed. They have often been criticized, however, because what comes out is nothing more than what went in. Conclusions can only articulate what is implicit in the given premises, and if the premises are not true, we wind up with a logical conclusion but inaccurate information.

Science no longer accepts self-evident axioms as a start in reasoning. Deductive logic is a frequent source of hypotheses, however, and the scientist often tests the internal consistency of his theories by setting them up in syllogistic form. It is not always clear to us what path a scientist's reasoning may take, but we often try to retrace his path with the laws of deductive logic; when we can't, we don't feel quite as safe in his presence.

Science is empirical; it is based on experience. An empiricist is one who believes that the source of knowledge is actual experience. He is somewhat like the proverbial man from Missouri who must be shown before he will believe. He uses the tools of inductive logic because he is not convinced that the laws of deductive logic are adequate. There is a joker in his deck of cards, however, and he can never prove by inductive logic alone that his conclusions are warranted. The sun has risen in the east throughout recorded history, but this fact alone does not prove that it will rise there tomorrow; it merely makes the event highly probable and no one should bet money to the contrary.

A great deal of time and energy has been wasted in debates on inductive versus deductive logic in science. The debates could have been avoided if the uses of both forms of logic had been recognized. Science is both rational and empirical. The laws of deductive logic must not be violated in the construction of theories and hypotheses, and the tools of inductive logic must be used in verifying them. Some sciences lean more heavily to the use of one system or the other, but all sciences have interwoven the two to such an extent that no further time should be wasted in trying to classify any science as either rational or empirical.

Science is objective; its findings are public property. The one distinctive characteristic of the charlatan is his claim to special knowledge. Unable to explain how or where he obtained his powers of understanding, he is nonetheless convinced that truth has been revealed to him and often to him alone.

Science is unable to accept subjective certitude as an adequate criterion of truth. Regardless of how intensely the scientist feels his knowledge is correct, the origins of that knowledge must be brought into the public domain. Neither privileged communication nor revelation is permissible in science. The scientist must specify the conditions under which he obtained his knowledge, and others of comparable training and experience must be able to duplicate his conditions and obtain the same knowledge. The scientist can only hope to be the first to discover truth; he can never be the only one.

Science is systematic; it proceeds by trial and error but not haphazardly. It has been traditional to define science as a systematized body of knowledge. If such a definition of science is adequate, then we must admit the telephone directory and the college catalogue to the realm of scientific knowledge. Systematic procedure is the characteristic most often identified with science by the general public, but it is not limited to science alone. A systematic survey may show that three out of four doctors recommended aspirin for headaches but this knowledge is hardly scientific. There would be less confusion about science perhaps if the general public—and television advertisers—used systematic where they often use scientific.

Trial and error in science does not imply random activity with the hope of stumbling on something. It implies rather that much of the scientist's efforts may be provisional. Luck has had a great deal to do with scientific discoveries but only because the scientist was in a position to catch the implications of an unexpected event. Far from being haphazard, the trials and errors of science may be carefully worked out in advance so as to cover all eventualities. In recent years science has become increasingly programmatic, meaning simply that scientific work is divided more and more carefully and planned further and further in advance.

Science is experimental; it specifies its conditions of observation. The classical design for a scientific experiment identifies three types of variables: the dependent, the independent, and the constant. The scientist is supposed to keep the lid on his constant variables, give the independent variable its head, and then watch the effect it has on the dependent variable. The design is neat and simple, but like virtue it is easier to define than to achieve.

The gist of experimental methodology is difficult to convey. Experimentation may range from crude trial and error to the elaborate manipulation and control of dozens of complex variables. Some form of control is almost always implied in experimentation and some form of manipulation may or may not be essential to the research design. The real heart of the experimental method, therefore, would seem to be that it is a means of research whereby the experimenter specifies the conditions under which he will observe certain events, arranges the conditions according to his specifications, and then observes or records the event he has designated as relevant.

Experimental methods are often criticized for being artificial. Modern science is dated, nonetheless, from the introduction of experimental methods of inquiry.

Science is quantitative; it counts and measures what it studies. Mathematics is intimately identified with science in the eyes of the general public, and the scientist may be visualized as a manipulator of complex mathematical equations almost as often as he is seen as operating weird laboratory equipment. But quantification in science implies considerably more than derivation of "the secret formula."

Measurement in science begins with the introduction of continuous variables which may be scaled in arbitrary but meaningful units. These permit a precision and accuracy unobtainable with broad, disjointed categories, and they provide a means of specifying how much as well as what. As science deals with more complex variables and relations, it becomes more and more dependent upon quantitative techniques to maintain the degree of precision and accuracy required.

Science is self-corrective; it can appeal to no outside authority. Having detached itself from established authority in the political, economic, and religious realms, science has not been anxious to establish its own. Somewhat similar to "the court of world opinion," it is an unusual kind of authority and may be described best in terms of checks and balances through a system of open discussion and criticism. The rules of science require that the scientist publicize his findings and that he give full particulars on theory, methods, and results. His findings then become part of the public domain and are subject to cross-questioning by any other member of the profession. Although no one is given final authority for a decision of validity or utility, it is expected that any errors made by the scientist in hypothesis, method of inquiry, and drawing of conclusions will be detected by his peers and that faulty interpretations will soon be replaced by more reliable ones.

The system has much to commend itself. The struggle with ignorance, prejudice, and superstition has been a long and bitter one, and scientists have no desire to replace one harsh master with another. The scientist may face years of uncertainty before a decision is rendered, but in science the accused are always given an opportunity to confront their accusers.

The 'Sine Qua Non' of Science

If we ask which of the above characteristics is most essential to science, we shall receive an ambiguous answer. Although each is a feature of scientific method, none is an absolute necessity. Experimentation is the most likely candidate for a *sine qua non*, but endorsement is more hesitant when we recall that astronomy has made great progress as a science in which experimentation is minimal. Control and manipulation of celestial bodies is quite impossible at our present stage of technology, but astronomy is nonetheless scientific. Anatomy, physiology, and other biological sciences have made great strides as sciences without the benefit of quantification; it is true that each has employed quantitative techniques more and more as it has progressed, but we cannot regard mathematical methods as essential.

No contemporary science is completely rational in the sense of using reason alone to acquire knowledge, and none should claim to be completely empirical. All sciences strive to be objective and systematic but these are not features exclusive to science. Nor is the characteristic of self-correction exclusive to science.

It would appear that all of the characteristics we have discussed are essential to science but they are not common to all sciences, and they may well be found in other areas of human endeavor. None can qualify as a *sine qua non*.

What then is the most distinctive feature or characteristic of science? If, as generally stated, science cannot be distinguished from other forms of intellectual inquiry by method, how can it be distinguished? The answer is that while method is essential to any definition of science, it will not suffice as its single distinctive feature; there are other ingredients which must be supplied—goals and assumptions.

The Goals
of Science

Although traditionally regarded as the goals of science, prediction and control are more properly considered the aims of technology. Science's objective is to understand and explain natural phenomena.

Prediction plays an unusually important part in science because there is no more stringent test of a scientific theory than to predict future events in such a way that the prediction can be verified. We can never quite be certain that a man's hindsight is scientific, but if he can specify in concrete, objective terms what some future event will be, we have a means of testing his foresight, and that is the genuine proof of his scientific pudding. Indeed, there is a delightful legend that science was born on May 28, 585 B.C. at 6:13 P.M. The event was an eclipse of the sun which had been predicted by an Ionian astronomer named Thales. No lucky stroke of prophecy was responsible for the birth of science at that particular time. It was the way in which Thales made his prediction, as well as the fact that his prediction was verified. Thales' prediction was scientific in that he had observed the regularities of the earth and moon, had formulated a law, and had tested his law by predicting an event which did in fact happen. This is the earliest known scientific prediction in history and if the legend is not quite true, the precision with which it is stated is characteristic of the knowledge scientists seek.

Prediction of the future, however, is a test that few sciences can meet as well as astronomy. While it is the best means we have of testing scientific hypotheses, it is more often desired than achieved. In other areas of science where the variables are more complex, we are seldom able to predict the future in as dramatic a fashion as Thales, but this does not lessen too severely our ability to understand and explain. The seismologist understands and explains earthquakes but he does not predict them; and the economist can often explain a depression but he doesn't predict one without contradiction from his colleagues.

We may temporarily leave to others the question of whether control is ever a proper objective of science. Technology definitely seeks to control the forces of nature whenever it can, and the progress of civilization is often measured by man's increasing control of his environment. This does not answer the question of science's pursuit of control, however, and it is well to bypass the issue if we can. Many scientists have expressed a preference to pursue knowledge and wisdom without regard for application to either the welfare or discomfort of human beings. Others have shown pangs of conscience where their work has led to discomfort and are seeking better voice in the uses of their discoveries and inventions. This conflict between science and technology is a problem with little hope of immediate solution.

Granting that the goals of science are understanding and explanation, we may next ask just how science proposes to explain the events it studies. The answer here is not always pleasing to poets, philosophers, and theologians. Yet, their dissatisfaction with science's efforts to explain natural events is due primarily to the fact that science poses a different kind of question. The scientist has learned from bitter experience that the questions he is permitted to ask is dependent upon the ends or values he has chosen. He recognizes that science can not answer questions of final causation or ultimate utility, and he seeks diligently to avoid questions that raise verbal issues rather than factual ones. He has learned that some questions are meaningful in the sense that factual answers can be obtained and that other questions are meaningless in that no criteria of an adequate answer are available. The scientist has chosen not to ask questions for which there are no standards by which an answer can be evaluated; he has agreed to ask only questions that can be adequately answered.

The reason the scientist's questions can be answered is that he does not ask "Why?" His questions are phrased in functional terms and permit answers in the form of statements describing how one observed event is related to another. When a relationship of this kind is of sufficient generality, it may be regarded as a scientific law.

In brief, then, science seeks to understand and explain by establishing functional relationships between observed entities and events. A scientific law may be said to be a statement of an invariant relationship between two or more variables. This implies that the entities and events observed by the scientist may change from occasion to occasion but that the relationship between the entities and events does not. An example may be seen in the simple formula, $C = \pi d$. This equation, when we are talking about physical circles (i.e., those actually drawn), is a scientific law in that it expresses a relationship between the circumference of a circle and its diameter. Both the circumference and the diameter will vary, of course, from circle to circle, but if the circles are correctly drawn, the relationship will always remain the same. The relationship between the two is expressed by the constant, π, which means simply that the circumference of a circle is always 3.14 times larger than the diameter. The equation consists, therefore, of two variables and one constant, and because curved lines are difficult to measure, it has an extremely useful application when we are confronted with the problem of measuring the circumference of a circle.

Having established an invariant relationship between the circumference and the diameter, the scientist believes that he has "explained" an important characteristic of circles. He has not told all we need to know about circles, but he has told us something important. Not all scientific laws, needless to say, are as simple as this one because other objects and events studied by scientists are not as simple as a circle. Yet, this simple relationship is a good example of the kind of relations sought by scientists, and it might be instructional to contrast it with Einstein's much publicized equation, $E = mc^2$, a functional relationship between two variables, involving a single constant.

Before leaving the scientist and his circle, it is well to reemphasize that he derived his scientific law only by asking the right questions; he did not make the mistake of asking, "Why does a circle have a circumference?"

The Assumptions of Science

The assumptions underlying scientific inquiry are numerous, but at least four should be recognized by those who seek an under-

standing of modern science. These four assumptions may be identified as: (1) determinism or natural causation, (2) finite causation,
(3) the principle of parsimony, and (4) the necessity of approximation and correction.

The first assumption implies simply that events are determined;
they don't just happen. It further implies that the causes of events
are natural phenomena occurring prior to or simultaneously with
them. The assumption rejects any notion of supernatural or metaphysical causation and is nothing more than a commitment to seek
an answer within the framework of natural science.

The second assumption is a recognition that a single event may
have more than one cause but that the number of these causes are
necessarily limited. We are well aware that a great deal is going
on at the same time and even the simplest event will have numerous antecedents. More than one of these antecedents may be necessary to explain the event, but, for the sake of economy, we reject
the notion that everything that ever went before is responsible.

In the third assumption the scientist promises himself and others
that he will not insist on a complex, involved, elaborate explanation of an event when a simple, direct one will suffice. This is a
rejection of excessive or unnecessary theorizing and a reaffirmation
of the scientist's willingness to proceed from the simple to the
complex. Like any other worker he may begin in the middle, but
here we are asking him to explain his work in terms of what went
before and not what comes after.

Finally, it would seem necessary to recognize that the work of
science will never be complete. Science seeks an approximation of
truth which it will gladly revise in the face of new evidence.
Scientists are aware of science's incompleteness and recognize the
need for continuous revision of its theories, laws, and hypotheses.
The willingness to revise, modify, change, and alter is necessary
for any scientist who would not degenerate into a dogmatist.

The 'Modus Operandi' of Science

The foregoing discussion has tried to show that whatever the essential nature of science, it must be understood in terms of
methods, goals, and assumptions. Science may be defined, then, as

an effort to understand and explain natural phenomena by the use of certain methods and under the handicaps of certain assumptions. It is a demanding, exacting game which must be played according to the ground rules laid down, but it has shown a remarkable ability to change the rules as necessity dictates. Science is always becoming; its work will never be finished.

Although no effort is made here to give a job description for the occupation of scientist, it is well to point out that much scientific work is conducted within a context of theory and to the rhythm of three beats: hypothesis, test, and verification.

It is now customary to speak of theory as a scientific shorthand. The scientist uses theory to represent to himself and others his many facts and findings and their relationships to each other. It is a framework into which empirical findings are incorporated and it is judged by its usefulness. If it can incorporate new facts without undue stress or strain and if it suggests new hypotheses for the scientist to test, it is regarded as a good theory. It may become obsolete on short notice, but if it maintains scientific momentum, it is useful.

Hypotheses in science may range from the intuitive guesswork of an adventurous novice to elaborate theorems rigorously derived from a carefully articulated set of mathematically stated postulates. In either case it is the question that the scientist seeks to answer. As we have seen, the answer he gets will depend greatly on the way he formulates his question. It is literally true that the better his question, the easier it is to answer.

In more cases than not, a properly stated question or hypothesis will suggest its own test. The test may not always be economically or technically feasible but it is the other leg of the hypothesis. The scientist who hypothesizes but does not test is a half-scientist; the one who tests but does not hypothesize is a technician. And at this point we perhaps come as close to the *sine qua non* of science as we can—an irresistable urge to test an idea.

But having conceived and tested an hypothesis, the scientist must verify. This may mean another test, a series of tests, or a program of research, but it is the thankless task of check and recheck. It is the resistence to subjective certitude, the cautiousness to check once again, and a nagging uncertainty that strips science of its glamour and romance. Verification is the dirty work of science but it, too, is essential.

In closing our discussion of the philosophy of science, it may be well to emphasize the variability of science itself. Certainly, it is evident by this time that there is no such thing as *the* scientific method which can be applied to any problem. The ground rules of science are explicit and flexible, but they are by no means infallible. Like any game of skill, science is played well by some and poorly by others. Scientists must be commended, however, for their tolerance of inferior players. It seems, therefore, that a distinctive feature of our many physical, biological, and social sciences might well be regarded as their level of sophistication. Some sciences are quite skilled in application of scientific methods, articulation of goals, and recognition of assumptions; others are just learning. Ranked by level of sophistication, physics appears, by consensus, to have won the title of our most sophisticated science. No nominations for the least sophisticated science need be made; the competition is too stiff.

Psychology As A Science

Having learned something of the distinctive characteristics of science, shall we now ask how scientific psychology is? As we have seen, an answer to this question depends upon how we define science. Most observers of contemporary psychology will readily agree that psychology is empirical, systematic, and experimental. Psychologists show an increasing skill in the application of quantitative techniques to psychological problems, and they display an increasing sophistication concerning the uses of deductive logic in theory construction.

Actually, as we shall see in our later discussion, there is no longer any serious question concerning psychology's status as a science. The investigation of behavior is definitely amenable to scientific methods; psychologists have accepted the restrictions (and advantages) of the assumptions under which scientists labor, articulated goals that are scientifically meaningful, and achieved, in general, a commendable level of scientific sophistication.

Some Historical
Antecedents of
Psychology   3

Psychology, like most other sciences, is better understood when we know something of its family background. The respectability of one's parents is no trivial matter in a world of social consciousness, and psychology, like others who have newly arrived, has shown no little concern with genealogy. There was a time when psychology, like many another parent-shy adolescent, sought to disavow its parentage. It was extremely intolerant of parental shortcomings, and assertions of autonomy and independence were made in ritualistic fashion. That psychology can now recognize parental virtues as well as parental vices is indicative of its maturity.

The Convergence of
Philosophy and Physiology

The establishment of psychology as a natural science is attributed to the convergence of philosophy and physiology upon a common set of problems. As physiology became better schooled in knowledge of the human organism's structure, it encountered problems of function. Philosophy, becoming more and more concerned with the problem of how we know the external world, began looking wistfully at the physiologist's knowledge of sense organs and neural conduction. By the middle of the nineteenth century, both had reached something of an impasse. The physiologist could no longer continue to learn about anatomy and neurology without asking embarrassing questions about their implications for human thought and conduct. Philosophy, on the other hand, could go no further with its inquiry if it hoped to be of any usefulness to society.

The impasse of philosophy was more critical. Early in the nineteenth century it had become apparent that philosophical efforts to unravel the knots of the mind-body dilemma were fruitless. In order to produce better results, philosophy had divided its labor: logic sought laws of thought and reasoning; aesthetics dealt with the nature of beauty; and epistemology tried to establish the origins and foundations of knowledge. Problems offering less hope for solution were exiled to metaphysics to be fussed over by those inclined to hairsplitting. Psychology had been given window dressing as mental philosophy but like metaphysics, its tools and instruments were speculation, intuition, and low-grade revelation. Students of mental philosophy were still losing sleep over inconsistencies between a world of reality and a world of appearance, and there was much busywork in cataloguing faculties of the mind to explain man's diverse behavior. It is fortunate that psychology was not dependent upon this branch of philosophy for parentage; there is too much suspicion that it was sterile.

BRITISH EMPIRICISM

René Descartes (1596–1650) was a French philosopher, mathematician, physicist, and physiologist but he is a logical beginning for the branch of philosophy known as British empiricism. In fact, Descartes is a logical start for many topics of interest in western civilization. He, more than anyone else, reintroduced the dualism of mind and body to western thought and then sought the best of both worlds. As a student of science he was well aware of the scientific revolution in progress during the seventeenth century and he made a sizable contribution himself by laying the foundations for analytical geometry. As a student of the mind, however, he sought to conserve free will in a world of physical determinism. His division of the two worlds was not clean-cut, and he introduced a third point of view by postulating that mind and body interacted in the pineal gland. Just how they transacted business there was not clear, but Descartes' compromise permitted him to pursue both lines of intellectual inquiry and made him the father of two opposing points of view of human nature—the mechanistic view that behavior is explicable in terms of physical mechanics and the interactional view that mind and body have a mutual influence over each other. His agility in this respect had the added advantage of keeping him out of trouble with ecclesiastical authority.

British empiricism, as a school of philosophy, began with the rejection of Descartes' notion of innate ideas. Thomas Hobbes (1588–1679) held the view that sensations were the source of knowledge and that higher mental processes could be accounted for by the association of ideas. Memories were declining images of past sensations, and imagination was a combination of sense impressions through association. Hobbes' view was strictly materialistic; reality was matter-in-motion and sensation was "commotion in the brain."

Hobbes' principles were extended by John Locke (1632–1704) who is best remembered for his comparison of an infant's mind to a blank sheet of paper. His comparison was an emphatic denial of innate ideas and a strong assertion that all knowledge is derived from experience. He sought to prove the empirical basis of knowledge by a distinction between characteristics that are inherent in the physical stimulus and those that are dependent upon the perceiver. But even Locke left the door open for further contributions from mind by means of a reflective sense—something vaguely similar to Descartes' innate ideas.

The school of British empiricism is traditionally continued by the works of George Berkeley (1685–1753), David Hume (1711–1776), and the Mills, James (1773–1836) and John Stuart (1806–1873). Each extended the principles of empiricism and associationism as sources of human knowledge, but none of them actually appealed to experience for an answer to their many problems. Although they advocated empiricism, they were quite rational in their approach, and they demonstrate in a cogent manner the futility of rationalism as a single method of inquiry. Berkeley's extension of Locke's reasoning led him to a solipsism in which mind was the only reality; Hume went further and abolished mind altogether but was stuck with disassembled contents like ideas, memories, and imagination. Hume was able to reconstruct complex ideas of memory and imagination by exercising the laws of association, but when James Mill extended Hume's concepts to their logical extreme, it was obvious that mental chemistry was at an impasse also.

John Stuart Mill restored better balance to the school, but despite the fact that the notion of mind had been altered radically by the empiricist-associationistic tradition, the mind was still encapsulated. British empiricism had undermined the dogmatism of rationalism, however, and it had turned philosophy to consideration of sensory processes and perception. It had focused on the problem of constructing mind from sensory experience, and the time was now ripe for an empirical approach to the problems of empiricism.

EXPERIMENTAL PHYSIOLOGY

Galen, the famous Roman physician, made a distinction between sensory and motor nerves as early as the second century. The distinction was not explicit, however, and religious opposition to dissection of the human body discouraged further inquiry until the Renaissance. At that time, both Leonardo da Vinci and Michelangelo dissected corpses to gain a better understanding of anatomy, and in 1543 Vesalius published his classic study, *De Humani Corporis Fabrica.*

With the introduction of experimental methods to the study of physiology, the distinction between sensory and motor nerves was reestablished in the early nineteenth century and thereby initiated a series of progressive leaps in neurology and physiology. The knowledge that sensory and motor functions were performed by different nerve fibers especially accelerated physiology's concern with function. The simultaneous discovery that neural conduction proceeded in only one direction suggested that man's behavior could be understood as a reflex. This gave a view of man as a reactive being and accounts for psychology's many efforts to explain behavior in terms of stimulus-response relationships.

The Bell-Magendie law, as the distinction became known, was followed by the experimental work of Johannes Mueller (1801–1858), who concluded that our perception of the external world does not depend upon the physical stimulus alone but depends also upon the sensory organ stimulated and the nature of neural conduction. Mueller postulated that each sensory nerve has a specific energy and that regardless of how the nerve is stimulated, it always gives rise to the same kind of sensation. Thus, the eye and the optic nerve can give us visual sensations only; we are never able to hear or to feel with them. Although Mueller's "doctrine of specific energies" is no longer generally accepted, the fact remains that the sensory modalities are unique.

One effect of Mueller's work was a phenomenon that we might call recession of the mind. Since the nerve fibers could be traced from the sense organs to the brain, the mind could no longer be localized in the body at large but must reside in the brain. Further substantiation of this point of view was found in concurrent studies on localization of function in the brain. In Scotland, Marshall Hall (1790–1857) had established that voluntary movement was a function of the cerebrum and that reflex movements were mediated by the spinal cord only. Hall's work was followed up by Pierre Flourens (1794–1867) in France, who demonstrated that the midbrain controlled visual and auditory reflexes, the medulla controlled respiration and heartbeat, and the cerebellum controlled coordination. Almost as important as Flourens' findings were his techniques of experimentation. The procedure, known as ablation, was to study the relationship between structure and function by selective removal of parts of an animal's brain through surgery. If postremoval tests revealed a change in the animal's behavior, then the extirpated part was deemed related to the function. Ablation techniques are still employed in the study of the relationship between brain functions and psychological functions, such as sensory discrimination, motor response, learning, and problem solving.

Two other innovations in techniques were made in mid-century by Paul Broca (1824–1880), who is given credit for discovery of a speech center in the brain, and by Fritsch (1838–1927) and Hitzig (1838–1907), who explored the cerebral cortex with electrical stimulation. Broca's method was called clinical in that observation of a patient who could not speak clearly was followed by an autopsy of the patient's brain after his death. Discovery of a lesion in the patient's cortex convinced Broca that a particular portion of the cortex controlled speech, and the area has become known as "Broca's area."

Fritsch and Hitzig's use of weak electrical currents to stimulate the cerebral cortex and thereby elicit motor responses was further proof that functions were localized in the brain and that the higher mental processes could be investigated by studying their underlying neural mechanism. Fritsch and Hitzig's techniques have become the most important means of studying brain functions but the mind is still receding. For a while it was evident that it resided in the cortex, but the search has been extended in recent years to subcortical regions.

No discussion of experimental physiology in the nineteenth century would be complete without mention of Franz Joseph Gall (1758–1828) and J. G. Spurzheim (1776–1832). Although remembered as phrenology and castigated as nonsense, their work was the first systematic effort to relate behavioral functions to neurological structure. The basic premise of their system, that variation in function signifies variation in structure, is still posited today, but time has demonstrated all too well how premature their efforts were.

Both Gall and Spurzheim were responsible for discoveries in neurophysiology, but they erred greatly in assuming a simple correlation between mental faculties and structural features of the brain. They were among the first neuroanatomists to designate the brain as the organ of mind, and they were also first to posit that the brain was composed of separate and independent organs. Perhaps no other topic shows as well how science and nonsense may run parallel and how thin the line of demarcation between the two may be at times. But more importantly, Gall and Spurzheim's work convinced other investigators that the mind-body issue in science had become one of relating function to structure and that efforts to investigate the relationship within the framework of natural science were long overdue.

The Experimental Effort

If Gall and Spurzheim had been better versed in experimental methods, we might have been spared their worst errors. Gall apparently began his studies with casual observation and once committed to his system evidently saw only what supported his thesis. That he could devote such good observational techniques to his study of anatomy and physiology and such poor ones to his study of mental processes is paradoxical. Although attacking phrenology on a different level of discourse and with experimental methods unsuited for adequate tests of Gall's premises, Pierre Flourens' rebuttal of Gall and Spurzheim's arguments demonstrated that issues in science must be submitted to arbitration by experimentation. His experiments did not prove Gall and Spurzheim wrong, but they did convince others that experimentation was the way to settle arguments.

THE WORLD OF PSYCHOPHYSICS

Credit for first applying experimental methods to psychological problems may be given to a German physiologist named Ernst

Weber (1795–1878). Weber's contribution stemmed from his interest in the functioning of sense organs. In investigating the sensitivity of "the muscle sense" to differences in weight, Weber established that his subjects responded to the relative differences of weights and not to their absolute magnitudes. He further established that the relative difference that could be detected by his subjects tended to be a constant ratio between the two weights. In short, in order to perceive the difference between one weight and another, the second weight had to exceed the other by a relative amount rather than an absolute one. Weber set this ratio for lifted weights at 1/40 and labeled the fraction, "a just noticeable difference." This implied that his subjects were able to detect a difference between a 40 and a 41 gram weight but not between an 80 and an 81 gram weight.

Weber's law, as it has become known, was the first precise relationship established between subjective experience and physical measurements. Weber fractions were later established for other sensory modalities, such as audition, pressure, smell, and taste, each of which is an unusually good example of the kind of knowledge which can be acquired only through experimentation.

Gustav Theodor Fechner (1801–1887), another versatile German of the day, saw in Weber's work something approaching a universal bridge between the mental and physical worlds. He concluded that if the ratio of a detectable increment and its original stimulus was a constant, then the "just noticeable difference" was a unit of sensation which could be used to correspond with units of physical measurement. He further concluded that mind and body were thereby identical, and he derived his own law which stated that the intensity of sensation was proportional to the common logarithm of the intensity of the stimulus. This implied that sensations increased in arithmetic form, taking steps of equal size, while the physical stimulus had to be increased geometrically, taking steps of increasing size.

Neither Weber's law nor Fechner's law has proved to be as universal as first supposed. The relationship between sensation and physical stimuli has been found to hold only within a limited range, and the subjective experience has been shown to be influenced by physical dimensions other than those implied by Fechner's law. The Weber-Fechner relationship is at best an approximation, and its contribution to psychology has been the stimulation it has provided.

Fechner is rightly regarded as the father of quantitative methods in psychology, however, because of the experimental methods he introduced. The three methods he perfected to study differential thresholds are still used in psychophysical experiments. Known as the method of average error, the method of constant stimuli, and the method of limits, these techniques have become standard procedures in psychological laboratories and may be regarded as part of the initiation rites of experimental psychologists.

FOUNDING OF WUNDT'S LABORATORY

Few introductory textbooks in psychology fail to tell us that Wilhelm Wundt (1832–1920) founded the first laboratory for psychological research at the University of Leipzig in 1879. American psychologists of nationalistic bent like to point out that William James set up a laboratory at Harvard University prior to Wundt's but they usually concede that James' laboratory was for demonstration purposes only.

Wundt was a good choice for psychology's man on horseback. Well versed in physiology, logic, aesthetics, physics, and metaphysics, he was quite skilled in working both sides of the street. A scholar of no small degree, Wundt's output of psychological material is said to come to 54,000 pages. Even considering that he lived for eighty-eight years, Wundt's publication pace is not maintained by any modern psychologist.

When the extent of Wundt's program is fully appreciated, it is well that his knowledge was encyclopedic and that his life was long. Wundt meant nothing less than the full-scale launching of a new science. Psychology was to be the science of experience; it would employ the methods that had proven fruitful in physiology and physics; and it was to be established as an experimental science with measurable stimuli and responses. Neither the soul nor mental faculties were to be a problem to psychology because both were irrelevant to its purposes. Psychology's objective would be to analyze consciousness, the immediate experience of the experiencing person. Exterior conditions would be varied according to the principles of experimental science and the content of consciousness would be described in terms of elements such as sensations, images, and feelings. The major method of investigation would thus be introspection—the observation and description of the contents of consciousness.

Wundt recognized the limitations of introspection as a laboratory method but he sought to overcome these as much as possible by using only subjects who were skilled in self-observation. In that way, he hoped that they would report only what was in their consciousness and not what they inferred from the stimulus situation. Mind, to Wundt, was a process—a conscious process, to be sure—but not an entity. Consciousness was the unity of sensation, feeling, and volition, and apperception—something strangely like a mind within a mind—was a means of assimilating and synthesizing experience. Wundt was not certain that the so-called higher mental processes could be studied experimentally but he believed that they could be studied by their products. Language, customs, beliefs, traditions, social institutions, law, and culture, in general, were products of man's higher mental processes and by studying these the psychologist could interpret the human mind in all its dimensions. The method was somewhat indirect but not unlike those used in later years.

From the vantage point of the twentieth century, the founding of Wundt's laboratory does not appear earth shaking, but it did establish psychology as an independent science. Although Wundt separated psychology from both philosophy and physiology, he continued the empirical-associationistic tradition begun by the British philosophers. His view of the mind-body problem was basically a philosophical one, and his efforts to analyze consciousness were still akin to mental chemistry.

EBBINGHAUS' STUDIES IN MEMORY

Fechner's development of psychophysical methods to study the relationship between subjective experience and physical measurements convinced others that mental processes themselves might be studied by experimental methods. One such person was Hermann Ebbinghaus (1850–1909) who published in 1885 his classic study of memory. Ebbinghaus' study is a landmark in the history of psychology for several reasons. Not only did he establish principles of learning and retention, which are valid today, but he displayed an ingenuity in reseach methods that is still to be envied. Recognizing the need for suitable materials to use in his experiments, Ebbinghaus reduced the influence of previous experience by inventing nonsense syllables. These were combinations of two consonants and a vowel arranged in such a way that they would have little resemblance to actual words. Ebbinghaus coined hundreds of such syllables and arranged them in lists of varying length to be memorized.

Working in a completely new area of inquiry, Ebbinghaus had to devise his own rules of procedure. He set as a criterion of mastery one errorless repetition of a list, and then having achieved this criterion for various lists of comparable length, he varied the intervening period before attempted recall. In this way he was able to establish relationships between the degree of learning and the amount of retention over a period of time. The fact that Ebbinghaus used himself as both experimenter and subject is further tribute to his ingenuity. Not only did Ebbinghaus demonstrate in delightful fashion that the higher mental processes of learning and memory were amenable to experimental inquiry, but he contributed methods and procedures of research which are still employed.

Systems, Schools, and Scholars

Although traditionally dated from the establishment of Wundt's laboratory in 1879, the initiation of psychology as a natural science was extended throughout most of the nineteenth century. Once separated from the restrictions of mental philosophy, psychology displayed a commendable capacity for growth, and soon after the turn of the twentieth century it began to sound much like a brash adolescent who had the answer to everything.

The turn of the century was accompanied by a flurry of events which were isolated and sometimes little regarded, but all were to find their way into the mainstream of psychology. Several of these developments, such as Francis Galton's (1822–1911) studies in England of individual differences and the concern with abnormal psychology in France, were concurrent with the work of Fechner, Wundt, and Ebbinghaus. A number of events highly significant to the later development of psychology cluster around the year 1900.

In Russia a physiologist named Ivan Pavlov (1849–1936) was conducting his experiments on conditioning. Pavlov discovered that when a tone preceded the presentation of meat powder to a hungry dog, the sound of the tone alone would eventually elicit the salivary response. Pavlov's work on conditioning was obscured for a while by his more important studies on digestive processes, but conditioning, as a means of studying stimulus-response relationships, soon provided a framework for the interpretation of learned behavior.

In France a psychologist named Alfred Binet (1857–1911) devised an instrument for measuring the intelligence of children by assessing such mental processes as reasoning and judgment. By employing a diversity of tasks which could be performed by children at different age levels, Binet not only developed the first workable scale for measuring "general intelligence" but contributed a rationale for the empirical validation of psychological tests.

In America Edward L. Thorndike (1879–1949) displayed in 1898 an ingenuity only slightly less than that of Ebbinghaus in studying the trials and errors of cats in trying to escape from a puzzle box. Two years earlier at the University of Pennsylvania, a clinic—the first of its kind—had been established to "study and treat mentally and morally retarded children."

Each of these events was to have considerable impact upon the budding science of psychology. There was still much confusion concerning the proper aims, purposes, and methods for a science of psychology, and the following years were absorbed with what might be called "the great debate" of schools, but a new science had been launched and it was obviously here to stay.

STRUCTURALISM

In most respects the development of schools of psychology in the early twentieth century was a reaction against the narrow limitations of the school of structuralism. Wundt's scholarship and his laboratory at Leipzig had attracted students from all corners of Europe and America. One of these was an Englishman named Edward Bradford Titchener (1867–1927). After earning his Ph.D. degree at Leipzig in 1892, Titchener migrated to the United States where he accepted an appointment to the faculty of Cornell University and there proceeded to emulate his former master.

Unlike other sciences and most systems of psychology, structuralism was directly dependent upon the experiencing subject. Physics was as much concerned with physical dimensions of the stimulating situation as psychology was, but only structuralism was exclusively concerned with the effect of the physical stimulus upon the experiencing subject.

To Titchener, who refined more than he altered Wundt's system, mind was the total sum of mental processes occurring in an individual's lifetime. Consciousness was the sum of mental processes occurring at any given time and the purpose of introspection was to analyze those processes. Perceptions were to be broken down into the elements of sensation, ideas resolved into images, and emotions analyzed as affections. Titchener substituted attention for Wundt's mysterious apperception, and he added two attributes to Wundt's original two. In short, the contents of consciousness were sensations, images, and affections, each of which could vary in quality, intensity, duration, and clearness—except affections which appear to have lacked clearness.

Psychology under Titchener was a descriptive science. Subjective experience was to be described in mentalistic terms but not explained by mental concepts; for causal explanations, psychology must refer to physiology. On this point, however, Titchener was extremely vague because he had stated clearly that consciousness parallels nervous processes in the brain but one does not cause the other. Titchener had also said that structure exists prior to function and must be understood before function can be explained. Here he meant the structure of consciousness, however, and not the structure of the nervous system.

Introspection, as a method of empirical science, just never quite came through to the skeptics. Titchener contended that introspection was valid only when conducted by skilled, well-trained subjects. This excluded children, animals, the mentally incompetent, and skeptics, no doubt, from service as subjects, but because some interesting contents might be present in their consciousness, Titchener permitted "introspection by analogy"; he shouldn't have because his critics never let him forget it.

Introspection called for specially trained subjects because the naïve are unusually susceptible to "the stimulus error." This was the nightmare of every good structuralist and meant simply that the subject had described the physical stimulus rather than his conscious experience. It seems that the introspecting subject was supposed to be something of an impressionistic painter; he wasn't supposed to tell what he saw but how he saw it.

But introspection failed for reasons worse than the stimulus error. It failed because the content of consciousness was so much more than passive, neutral sensations and images of physical objects. The flow of consciousness is an active process, often filled with intense feelings like hate, love, and anger, which have a way of disappearing when the subject turns his objective, scientific inner eye to them. Intense feelings can be described in retrospect but it is never quite the same.

Titchener never fulfilled Wundt's program for psychology. Wundt's dual objectives for the science of psychology were to analyze consciousness and then to discover the laws of synthesis. Not only was mind to be analyzed in the best manner of mental chemistry but it was to be reconstructed out of the elements it identified. The outcome of structuralism was that it had succeeded in breaking mind to pieces but it could provide no clues for reconstruction. Structuralism, as a school of psychology, closed with mind in a Humpty-Dumpty condition; the problem was what to do with all the egg shells.

FUNCTIONALISM

Historical perspective suggests that structuralism never really found a home in America. It was a German import made by an Englishman, and it never actually appealed to home folks. Although Titchener attracted many students to Cornell, their allegiance appears to have been to the man and not to the system. In fact, Titchener himself apparently outlived structuralism by almost a decade.

The American brand of psychology had long been brewing and eventually it became known as functionalism. As a school of psychology, functionalism could claim two distinguished founders, William James (1842–1910) and John Dewey (1859–1952), but its characteristics never became as sharply defined as those of structuralism and the other schools of the day. The underlying philosophy of functionalism was influenced greatly by Darwin's theory of evolution, and it found a sympathetic climate in America for much the same reasons that evolutionary theory did.

Functionalism began as a conscious imitation of the experimental and physiological approach which was being made at the same time in Germany. It is best understood, however, as a revolt against the sterility of structuralism as an explanation of human behavior. To American psychology, the matter of importance was not the organism's state of consciousness but its efforts to adjust to the environment. William James believed that psychology should study consciousness but as an ongoing process. To him, mind was in continuous interaction with environment, and he believed that its content and characteristics were best revealed by the possessor's habits and knowledge. As the name of the school implies, mind was functional; its structure was of little help in explaining the activity of the organism.

Functionalism never became highly systemized and it is sometimes difficult to see just how it qualifies as a school of psychology. Its major characteristic seems to have been an attitude of flexibility and a concern with adaptive behavior. Psychology would be defined by many functionalists as the study of mental activity, as opposed to the structuralist's study of mental content. But while the functionalist's attitude toward mind was flexible, he was interested in mental activity only if it enabled him to understand the acquisition, retention, and application of "experiences." Both mind and body were proper fields for study, but resolution of the mind-body problem was a task for philosophy.

The more the functionalists became concerned with adaptive behavior, the more they shifted their attention to problems of learning. If the significant event in psychology was the organism's efforts to adjust to its environment, then psychology should study the modifiability of behavior. This implied that introspection was limited as a method of inquiry. The kind of behavior which interested the functionalist becomes less and less accessible to consciousness as it develops. The functionalist pointed out that a motor skill is very much a conscious process in its initial stages of learning but as the skill is perfected, it becomes less conscious. Consequently, the subject may perform highly complex tasks without any conscious awareness. Objective observation rather than introspection gave the functionalist a better view of what was going on. It also permitted him to use animals and children as subjects and to benefit from observation of simpler forms of behavior.

The fact that functionalism developed under numerous leaders with varied interests and different backgrounds accounts to no little degree for its viability. Structuralism in America had become the exclusive property of a single, influential leader, who succeeded so well in systematizing his point of view that diversity was not possible. Functionalism was always open to suggestion and this, as we shall see later, accounts for the fact that it survived while other systems failed.

BEHAVIORISM

It would be a mistake to conclude that all American psychologists were satisfied with the state of affairs in functionalism. One dissatisfied psychologist was John B. Watson (1878–1958), who founded the school of behaviorism. Watson had been trained in psychology at the University of Chicago where functionalism sat enthroned, but he never found functionalism a satisfactory point of view. His early work with animals apparently convinced him that neither functionalism nor structuralism could become an objective science because both were tainted with mentalism. In working with animals Watson felt no need for "introspection by analogy," and he soon concluded that psychology had no need for such mentalistic concepts as mind, consciousness, images, feelings, or sensations. It was possible to establish a science of behavior in which the psychologist studied behavioral acts in terms of stimulus and response. This would be a truly objective science and would not be weighted down with imagined, unseen events and processes supposedly taking place in the mind.

The aim of Watson's science of behavior would be to establish laws concerning the relationships between stimuli and responses in such a way that given the stimulus the psychologist would have no difficulty in predicting the response, and given the response he would be able to specify what the antecedent stimulus had been. Behaviorism was to accomplish this goal by studying habit formation—the process by which habits are acquired. Borrowing the concept of conditioned reflexes from Pavlov, Watson made conditioning a cornerstone of his system and rejected all notion of heredity as an explanatory construct. Behavior was the result of prior conditioning and the integration of reflexes into habits.

In order to test his theories of habit formation, Watson shifted his attention to research on children, and coming in a day when an unsentimental realism was current in art, literature, and drama, his notions on child-rearing achieved no little popularity. Watson is best remembered for his extreme environmentalism and his often quoted statement that he could train children to be what he wanted them to be. Actually, Watson's statement was far from being as extreme as posterity recalls. What he actually asked for was "a dozen healthy infants" and his "own specified world to bring them up in"; something about healthy children and his own specified world makes it easier for us to believe that he could actually deliver on his promise.

Having declared for an objective, mechanistic explanation of human behavior, Watson later found it necessary to moderate his views. Although he regarded emotional behavior as primarily visceral, he found it necessary to rely on verbal report for certain information. This, to be sure, was a poor substitute for objective observation but it still sounded a bit like introspection. Thinking was equated by Watson to subvocal speech; this implied that, theoretically, suitable recording devices could be attached to the subject's larynx and verbal report eventually dispensed with.

It is interesting that Watson resolved the mind-body or structure-function problem by casting out all notion of mind and all concern with structure. Psychology was still functional in that it sought relationships between antecedent conditions and observed consequences, but it concerned itself solely with observable behavior, and it admitted no notions of causation in the form of volition, desire, feelings, perceptions, or thought. The ghost in the central nervous system had been exorcised, and psychology could now settle down to its proper work of studying stimulus-response relations.

Watson's revolt against structuralism and functionalism impresses us today as being a little too radical. The accommodating attitude of the functionalists seems a better one for scientists, and Watson didn't sound as if he would permit any kind of compromise. The reason might well be that Watson's extreme viewpoint was necessary to shake psychology free of some of its old mentalistic habits. Another reason might be that Watson's stand was not as extreme as it first appeared. Too often in reading Watson we get the impression that by behavior he meant only the contraction of muscles and the secretion of glands. Yet, Watson himself thought that psychology as a science of behavior could contribute immensely to such fields as education, industry, and government. His own subsequent career in advertising suggests that his viewpoint was not as mechanistic as he would have us believe.

GESTALT PSYCHOLOGY

The German word *Gestalt* has no precise equivalent in English; it is usually defined as an approximation of the English concepts of pattern or configuration. Perhaps it would be better to say that *Gestalt* means organization because as the term was used by the Gestalt psychologists, it pertained more to the organization of experience than anything else.

Gestalt psychology was a reaction against structuralism, but because it found a more formidable rival in behaviorism, it quickly centered its arguments on the S-R theorists. Opposing all efforts to analyze experience into components, be they elements of consciousness or stimulus-response couplings, the Gestalt psychologists focused on perceptual phenomena as the most important event in psychology. As early as 1912 one of the founders of Gestalt psychology, Max Wertheimer (1880–1943), had pointed out that nothing in the school of structuralism could account for the illusion of movement when discrete visual stimuli are presented in rapid succession. This phenomenon, so common to us today in the moving arrows of neon signs, could not be analyzed by the structuralists, no matter how skilled they were at introspection, and even though they knew from manipulation of the physical correlates that the events were discrete, they were still subject to the illusion of movement. Alternating the exposure of light through two slits inclined 20 to 30 degrees apart, Wertheimer established that apparent movement was dependent upon the interval between presentations. If the interval was too long, the lights were seen successively; if too short, the lights were seen as continuous. Wertheimer concluded that our perceptions of the external world are dependent upon the pattern of stimulation and not the function of physical dimensions as the structuralists supposed. He went even further to point out that the elements of consciousness, as revealed by introspection, were artifacts and not elements out of which mind could be synthesized.

Wertheimer and his associates, Kurt Koffka (1886–1941) and Wolfgang Köhler (1887–   ), posited that the objective of psychology should be to derive principles of organization. They disagreed with the behaviorists about the undesirability of introspection and, by way of phenomenological analysis, reintroduced the experiencing subject to psychology. This implied that the subject matter of psychology was the world of appearance and that it was to be studied as given, not analyzed or reduced to other forms. The mind-body dilemma was resolved through the principle of isomorphism which implied that an inherent similarity existed between neural events and perceptual phenomena. In brief, our perceptions correspond to the external stimulus in much the same manner that a sound wave corresponds to the electrical impulse it sets up in a telephone transmitter. The two are different forms of energy but have the same form, pattern, or organization.

The Gestalt psychologists are best remembered for pointing out that the whole is greater than the sum of its parts. Gestalt theory has influenced greatly our notions of perception, learning, thinking, and problem-solving—but perception in particular.

The development of psychoanalytic psychology was a movement largely outside the mainstream of psychology. Its founder, Sigmund Freud (1856–1939), was a physician who had specialized in neurology and his development of psychoanalytic thought took place within the psychiatric setting. Freud began his work by using hypnosis to analyze and treat neurotic patients. Having studied under the French neurologist, Jean Marton Charcot (1825–1893), Freud had been much impressed with hypnotic facilitation of recall. He collaborated for a while with a German physician, Joseph Breuer (1842–1925), who had found that patients could be hypnotized, encouraged to talk out their difficulties, and relieved of troublesome neurotic symptoms. Freud made the not-so-amazing discovery that people were willing to talk about their troubles without being hypnotized, and he turned to diagnostic techniques of free association and analysis of dreams.

Freud's use of free association places him in the associationistic-empirical tradition. If functionalism and behaviorism can be regarded as movement away from structuralism in one direction, Freud's theories may be regarded as movement in the other. Structuralism, as the science of consciousness, had omitted such phenomena as hypnosis, dreams, and amnesia, and Freud early detected that by focusing exclusively on conscious experience, the structuralists were excluding the major part of mental activity. He became convinced that the more significant aspects of mental life were not available to consciousness. Through a process of free association, the patient could recall events which had long been suppressed and were unknown to the patient but which, nonetheless, had a bearing on his neurotic behavior.

Although Freud neither invented nor discovered the unconscious mind, his conception of unconscious motivation became the cornerstone of his theories. Whereas the functionalists had regarded the organism's efforts to adjust to environment as the significant event, Freud studied the conflict between the organism's instinctive urges and the restrictions of society. The individual was not trying to adjust to society; he was at war with it. But because society is a highly potent enemy, the conflict is internalized by the individual and becomes a struggle between the id, the pleasure-seeking component of man's mental structure, and the ego, the conscious, reality-governed component. In this way the individual is torn between conflicting impulses, many of which he can resolve only through repression.

The significant event in psychoanalytic psychology, therefore, is irrational conflict between instinctive forces within the individual's mind. Traumatic experiences early in the life of the individual are usually treated as the origin of these conflicts and despite the fact that the traumatic experiences may be repressed, the conflict goes on. Through the analysis of dreams and the use of free association as a means of facilitating recall, the psychoanalyst may observe the inner struggles between the ego and id.

Freud's theories of unconscious motivation imply a rigid psychological determinism. The process of analysis was one of rational understanding, supposedly based on empirical observation, but it focused on irrational forms of behavior and admitted no notions of accidental behavior. Man's behavior was irrational, but it was strictly determined in a highly rational manner.

Freud's theories began with the assumption that mental disorders, such as hysteria, are exaggerated expressions of psychological processes common to all men. His concern with the etiology and treatment of mental disorders was later channeled, however, into speculation about religion, history, and civilization in general. It is a bit ironic, therefore, that Freud's last works were efforts to construct a philosophy of life. In his early years Freud had been justifiably critical of the branch of philosophy known as German idealism; in his later years he attempted to construct an embarrassingly similar view of the world.

The Dissolution of Schools

The "great debate" among schools of psychology lasted for approximately twenty years. The most intensive stage was reached with salvoes between behaviorists, gestaltists, and psychoanalysts, but by the time of the early thirties, it had subsided into an affair of occasional pot-shooting. The debates had centered around the issues of mind-body, introspection, and the significant event. Each of the schools, as we have seen, was forced to grapple with these particular problems and each resolved them in its own manner. The structuralists and functionalists resolved the mind-body dichotomy by straddling it in a somewhat precarious manner, the behaviorists by casting out all notions of mind, and the psychoanalysts by probing the subterranean depths of mind; only the Gestalt psychologists provided an ingenious solution with their doctrine of isomorphism.

Each of the schools was plagued with the problem of accepting or rejecting the self-observation of its subjects. All sciences were becoming aware that in the final analysis they were all dealing with the experiences of man, but psychology had exclusive claim to the subjective, private, personal, or immediate experiences of the individual. The problem was what to do with these experiences. The psychologist was aware that other sciences had progressed only as they made their observations independent of the perceiving scientist; yet, the very nature of the processes in which the psychologist was interested made them unobservable in the same manner. The desire to be objective was handicapped greatly by the knowledge that psychology's subject matter was subjective.

The structuralists took full cognizance of the issue in defining psychology as the study of consciousness. They recognized the limitations of introspection as a method of inquiry but sought to reduce the limitations by training its subjects to observe and report their immediate experiences without contamination by inference, knowledge, or attitude. The functionalists preferred not to rely on self-observation but treated it as a sometimes necessary source of information. The attitude of functionalism was always ambivalent, however, and we may suspect that there was a bit of envy of behaviorism for taking its bold stand on the issue. The Gestalt psychologists wanted the subject's self-observations but without the contamination of structuralistic training. In short, they wanted the subject's naïve introspections, his subjective experiences as given. The psychoanalysts were also interested in the subject's self-observations but they contended that the subject needed the analyst's help in recalling the aspects of experience that were important. By engaging in free association under the analyst's guidance, the subject could bring to consciousness events which had been repressed and were thereby inaccessible to consciousness as studied by the structuralist. Only the behaviorists made a clean break with introspection. Taking a stand that they were interested in only what they could observe, the behaviorists pretended to be uninterested in anything the subject had to say about his own experiences.

The significant event in a science of psychology was the focal point of the psychologist's attention, and it would appear that the schools differed more in this respect than any other. To the structuralists, the significant event was the contents of consciousness; these were to be described, analyzed, and then synthesized in the tradition of analytic chemistry. The functionalists were concerned with the strivings of the organism to meet the demands placed upon it by its environment. The significant event to them was how the organism adapted to environmental demands. The psychoanalysts focused on the irrational conflict going on in the subject's unconscious. It was not the contents of consciousness that mattered most to them but rather the events which had been repressed and now sought reentry to consciousness in a disguised or symbolized form. The behaviorists wanted to study only the overt behavior of their subjects and the antecedent conditions. Their significant event was to take place neither in the dark recesses of an unconscious mind nor in the clear light of a conscious one; they wanted no part of internal events, but sought S-R links between the preceding events and the subject's overt behavior.

The debate between schools was lessened not by resolution of the basic issues that were dividing them, but rather by the subversive activities of empirical facts. In arguing what psychology was and what it ought to be, each of the schools presented empirical evidence in support of its point of view. As the debate continued, each antagonist began to show respect for his opponent's facts; intense feelings could still be aroused over the other man's explanation, but his facts were something else. The result was a borrowing of the other man's data without buying his explanation; the issues over which the schools had drawn blood remained, but they became less and less important in the face of such interesting facts as their proponents provided.

A View of
Contemporary
Psychology   4

If asked to describe American psychology in two words, we should be forced to reply that it is functionalistic and behavioristic. Does this mean then that the functionalists and the behaviorists have formed some kind of alliance and succeeded in demolishing their adversaries? No, it means simply that American psychology has shown a remarkable capacity for absorbing opposing points of view and a pronounced disinclination to become doctrinaire. It must be recalled that structuralism, psychoanalysis, and Gestalt psychology were all products of the German culture while functionalism and behaviorism were native to the soil. The functionalists did not reject the proposals of the structuralists *in toto;* they merely regarded structuralism as an incomplete psychology, and they sought to contribute knowledge in other ways by use of other methods. Behaviorism began as a revolt against functionalism, but it was the revolt of an energetic child against a permissive parent. Although functionalism had not always encouraged the research on animals that apparently led Watson to his rejection of mentalism, it is well to remember that Watson had been trained in the stronghold of functionalism.

If any school has triumphed over the others, it may be said that functionalism has triumphed by being less of a school than structuralism, behaviorism, psychoanalysis, and Gestalt psychology. In its concern with adaptive behavior, functionalism proved to be highly adaptive itself. It was willing to incorporate empirical data from any reliable source, and it did so without acquiring encumbersome doctrines. There was no real difficulty in reconciling its differences with behaviorism; all that the behaviorists had to do was to become a little more judicious and they were readily welcomed. Indeed, functionalism welcomed behaviorism at its own definition, and it is now traditional to define psychology as the science of behavior.

Nor did functionalism have a great deal of trouble with Gestalt principles of organization. Proponents of both schools had been all too aware of the limitations of structuralism, and there was more than a little harmony of interest in that respect. Quite able to appreciate the Gestaltist's concern with perception, the functionalists were influenced by Gestalt principles in learning and thinking. Fundamental differences between the two schools would persist— primarily because the functionalists were empiricist and the Gestaltists were nativistic—but the differences were not severe enough to maintain territorial integrity.

Of all opposing points of view, the functionalists appear to have been the most ambivalent toward the psychoanalysts. The basic differences between the two groups apparently stems from some fundamental disagreements about human nature and a disparity of philosophical antecedents. Imbued with a faith in environmentalism, inevitable progress, and material success, the American psychologist has been inclined to view the psychoanalytic concept of man as degrading. Freud's theory of infantile sexuality was unacceptable to men who had been raised to expect great things for their children. The American success story implied that life was good and the next generation would have it even better; father fixations and mother complexes just didn't fit. Moreover, the functionalists were always behavioristic enough to suspect that Freud's warring ids and egos were strangely animistic, and they could see little advantage to either internalizing mythology or fractionating the mind further. In America man struggled with and conquered his environment; he did not struggle with himself, and surely, he was not defeated by himself.

Still, the functionalists could accommodate many a psychoanalytic concept and they did so in a highly selective manner. Smuggled into the mainstream of American psychology, many contributions of psychoanalysis are now "common sense," a kind of gift from an unnamed donor. Psychoanalytic principles have achieved considerable popularity in American art, literature, and drama, but its relationship with American psychology is still one of strained toleration.

Should we conclude then that the basic issues play little part in contemporary psychology? Again, the answer is no. Despite much rapprochement among the various schools of psychological thought, the issues remain, but in a slightly different guise and with less intensity. Although no longer cast into the form of mind-body dualism, the issue of structure versus function is still with us. Psychologists describe behavioral functions and physiologists describe neurophysiological structure, but the levels of description are not on the same plane. Talk about reduction of psychological concepts to those of neurophysiology can still be spirited, as in the recent discovery of subcortical centers for emotions and motivation, but for the most part psychologists live with the issue and lose no sleep.

Psychologists no longer exclude self-observation as a source of information, but they do recognize its limitations and they avoid dependence upon its use whenever possible. As a method of observation, it must be checked by other methods; interestingly enough, however, it still is our main source of information about some of our most pertinent behavior, i.e., pleasure, pain, anger, grief, and love.

As for the significant event in psychology, it appears to have undergone the most radical change. No aspect of behavior is focused on to the exclusion of all others, and no one seeks to explain all behavior in terms of a single motif. The schools of psychology have been replaced by theories of learning, theories of perception, and theories of personality; those in turn are being reduced to miniature theories and constructed models. Like other sciences, psychology appears capable of dividing its work to infinite degrees.

Yet three fundamental or basic issues remain to provide a semblance of unity for contemporary psychology. These are the problems of perception, motivation, and learning, and they may be cast in philosophical form as the questions: "How do we know the external world?" "What makes us go?" "How do we modify our behavior?" Other questions will push to the focal point of psychological consciousness from time to time and many other questions remain to be answered before human behavior can be explained adequately. But perception, motivation, and learning are the gravitational centers of contemporary psychology and regardless of how often we are forced to detour, psychological roads have a way of leading back to these three problems.

There is no generally accepted psychological theory which considers all problems of perception, motivation, and learning, but none of the three sets of problems is treated independently of the other two. The relationships between the three may be represented best by a triangle with the three sides labeled perception, motivation, and learning. Such representation would imply that one set of problems blends directly into the other two. It would further suggest that one cannot be considered to the exclusion of the others. The interrelations of the three are indeed intimate. If, as the British empiricists claimed, all knowledge is derived from the external world, we must now recognize that our perception of the external world is quite dependent upon our previous experiences. And if, as is so often claimed, we must be motivated to learn, so must we recognize that we also learn to be motivated. No clean-cut divisions can be made on the inside of our triangle; it is unitary.

Nor should we at this time attempt to specify the shape of the triangle. Since we cannot yet determine the relative importance of each of the three, the triangle could turn out to be any conceivable triangular shape. One speculation may be ventured, however, about the base of the triangle; there is strong suspicion that it is properly labeled learning.

Explanation and Prediction in Psychology

We have seen that explanation in science is essentially a process of describing in generalized terms the conditions necessary for the occurrence of a particular event. An event is said to be explained when we have described its antecedent conditions in such a manner that we may regard the event as a logically necessary consequent. In other words, an event is explained when it can be deduced from or predicted by an established uniformity or regularity, i.e., a scientific law.

Critics of psychology frequently cast suspicion upon the predictability of human behavior by questioning the existence of invariant relationships which would qualify as scientific laws of behavior. One group of critics apparently dislikes the scientific posture of psychology because they believe that psychology cannot predict behavior and another group scorns psychology because they fear that it can. The first viewpoint compares psychology's success in prediction with that of the physical sciences and contends that until psychology can predict with a comparable degree of accuracy, we cannot have a science of behavior. The second point of view apparently equates notions of psychological determinism with philosophical fatalism and contends, more or less, that even if

psychology could predict human behavior it would be morally un-
desirable to do so.

Neither of these criticisms is a serious threat to psychology's
status as a science. Psychological determinism is by no means
equivalent to philosophical fatalism, and absoluteness of prediction is not a suitable criterion for scientific status. The complexity
of the variables in human behavior makes it most unlikely that any
individual's life is set on such an unalterable course that he must
live out his life regardless of changing circumstances or that we
may predict his every action without error. We must agree with
William James that psychology will never be able to write bio-
graphies in advance.

In many respects the current scientific status of psychology is
similar to that of meteorology. Both psychologists and meteorolo-
gists predict future events, but their predictions must be based on
contingencies beyond the control of the predictor. Both are correct
in their predictions more frequently than they are wrong but because of the high visability of their errors, the general public is
more inclined to remember the times when the weatherman and
the psychologist are wrong. Even in comparison with the weatherman, however, the psychologist is at a disadvantage. The weather
is uninfluenced by the predictions that have been made; the psychologist is not always certain that knowledge of predicted behavior
does not radically alter the behavior.

In brief, the explanation and prediction of behavior are based on
established relationships of functional dependence between observed behavior and its antecedent conditions. To understand psychological explanation and prediction, we must understand the
empirical relationships or laws established by psychologists, the
concepts they use in the description and regulation of psychological
variables, and their efforts to unify empirical relationships and
psychological concepts into a coherent theory of behavior.

PSYCHOLOGICAL LAWS

The search for empirical relationships in psychology has followed
two traditional paths. Psychologists in the associationistic-empirical
tradition seek to establish functional relationships between stimulus
variables and response variables. Despite the fact that they are
lumped together as S-R psychologists, this group presents a diversity of viewpoints concerning the nature and specificity of empirical

relationships in psychology. Their only common ground is an implicit agreement that psychology must rest on clearly demonstrated relationships between the antecedent variables stimulating the organism and the consequent behavioral responses of the organism.

The second group of psychologists seeks to establish empirical relationships between the responses of the organism in one situation and its responses in another; these psychologists seek what may be designated as R-R laws of behavior. For example, college applicants' scores on intelligence tests may be compared with their academic performance in college to determine the extent to which the two sets of responses are related; the responses given by subjects on a personality inventory may be related to performance on the job or adjustment to the community; or the subjects' responses to a questionnaire may be related to their performance on an experiment task explicitly designed to elicit certain types of behavior.

A third type of psychological law is frequently proposed by some psychologists. This type of empirical relationship pertains to the characteristics of the organism and its responses in a given situation and may be identified as O-R laws. The organismic variables may be characteristics such as age, sex, temperament, personality, body type, or they may be state variables such as the condition of the organism after the administration of a drug or after surgical preparation.

Actually, as increased familiarity with psychological research will show, there are numerous types of empirical relationships studied by psychologists. The schema, S-O-R, representing stimulus, organism, and response, suggests several other types of relationships which receive varying attention and investigation. Some learning and perception theorists are avowedly concerned with S-S relationships while some personality theorists appear to be exclusively interested in O-O relations. There is good reason to believe, however, that virtually all psychological laws may be effectively treated as either S-R or R-R laws.

PSYCHOLOGICAL CONCEPTS

Some psychologists believe that in its present status as a science psychology should be concerned only with the investigation and description of the functional dependence of one psychological variable upon another. In their view, it is sufficient to establish that two or more psychological variables are functionally related without endeavoring to specify the nature of the relationship.

Other psychologists believe that in any S-R or R-R law of behavior, the "dash" is the important component of the relationship and the proper subject for the psychologist's attention. They believe that the relationship must be accounted for by entities or processes that mediate the presentation of the stimulus and the observation of the response. To account for the relationship inferred between antecedent conditions and observed consequences, the psychologist devises symbolic concepts which he does not observe directly but which he infers from his control of stimulus and response variables.

The concepts used in psychology may be said to be either empirical or theoretical. Empirical concepts pertain to objects and events that are observable while theoretical concepts are employed to represent the relations among observable events and empirical concepts. For example, reinforcement is a concept frequently employed by psychologists. As an empirical concept, it may be defined operationally as the presentation of food (or some other "reward") in a learning experiment where the presentation of the food is contingent upon a specified response, such as the pressing of a bar by a rat.

The operational definition of reinforcement in this manner is a means of identifying the concept by reference to the set of operations involved in its use. The psychologist is saying, in effect, that when the rat presses the bar and receives a pellet of food, the presentation of the pellet of food is what he means as reinforcement. In short, by giving such an operational definition of reinforcement, the psychologist is specifying the rules which govern his use of the concept. Such a definition permits the psychologist to vary numerous conditions of reinforcement and to investigate the relationships between response acquisition and the concept of reinforcement. There are other ways in which reinforcement may be operationally defined, but all psychologically meaningful definitions of the concept must be specified by either observable objects and events or a set of operations.

To distinguish clearly between the empirical concepts that are reducible to observations and operations and the theoretical concepts which are inferred relations some psychologists refer to the latter as theoretical constructs—intending simply that the theoretical constructs are a special class of psychological concepts. Referred to variously as symbolic concepts, hypothetical concepts, or intervening variables, theoretical constructs are at least one step removed from empirical concepts which are in turn at least one step removed from the observations and operations of the psychologists. Theoretical constructs do not exist in the way that we think of physical entities and processes; they are devised solely to account for the events actually observed by the psychologist and, as such, they are merely instrumental to the explanation and prediction of behavior.

One example of a theoretical construct in learning theory is that of habit. As a theoretical construct, habit represents an inferred relationship between an observed response and the number of reinforcements the experimental subject has received in making the response. In the case of rats pressing a bar, we would infer that the habit strength of a bar pressing response is greater for a rat having received 100 reinforcements than for a rat having received only 40 reinforcements. The construct of habit is, therefore, a convenient way of expressing the conditions of a previously acquired response.

It is obvious that the use of theoretical constructs is fraught with some difficulty. Because the psychologist uses the term habit to represent the conditions of response acquisition and because habit is used frequently in common speech, it is easy to misunderstand the psychologist's use of the term. It should be clear that he is not using the term in the same way that the layman does when he speaks of "the smoking habit" or "the bad habits" he acquired from the older boys in his neighborhood. The psychologist has made an effort to define his term habit rigorously and to limit his use of the term to the observations, operations, or relationships designated. He rejects any notion of habit as an entity or a thing-in-itself, and he seeks to avoid the metaphysical status that the layman may be inclined to assign the concept. Habit is not the *cause* of the observed behavior; it is a convenient way of specifying how the behavior developed.

Other theoretical constructs, such as IQ, expectancy, self, ego, drive, and anxiety are used in a similar manner. In no case are these constructs things-in-motion or faculties of the mind; in all cases, however, they are tools of thought devised by the psychologist to identify psychological relationships. Lest we appear to belabor this point, it is well to remember that a necessary phase of scientific reasoning is to devise abstractions which are capable of generalization to phenomena other than that from which the abstractions are drawn. The theoretical constructs of the psychologist are no more abstract than those of the physicist, chemist, or biologist; their sole purpose is to account for as many empirical relationships as possible and to facilitate the warranted prediction of events which have not yet occurred.

Psychological Theory and Research

As mentioned previously, the schools of psychology have been superceded by theories limiting explanatory constructs and empirical findings to areas of behavior such as learning, perception, and motivation. This division of labor has permitted more systematic inquiry into specific topics and resulted in greater effectiveness in both explanation and prediction.

Theories of psychology serve numerous purposes. The most important purposes of psychological theories, however, are to (1) delineate the area of inquiry, (2) specify the problems of investigation, (3) summarize the existing knowledge in the area, (4) suggest productive lines of inquiry, and (5) indicate applications and interpretations of the knowledge acquired.

Although psychologists occasionally disagree as to the level of sophistication psychological theory, in general, has achieved, they recognize the varying levels attained within the different areas of inquiry. Current psychological theories vary greatly in (1) degree of formality—the extent to which the theory can be formulated as a deductive system; (2) comprehensiveness—the capacity to incorporate the empirical findings of research; (3) predictive power—the ability to predict future events; (4) hypothetical richness—the capacity to generate meaningful hypotheses for empirical testing; and (5) sensitivity to empirical evidence—the ease with which the theory can assimilate new data or research findings.

THEORIES OF LEARNING

Current theories of learning have been influenced by the schools of behaviorism, functionalism, and Gestalt psychology. The majority of learning theorists accept Watson's methodological point of view, but not in the behaviorist sense of denying the existence and usefulness of a conscious mind. They believe that learning must be studied as overt behavior, and they employ rigorously defined theoretical constructs rather than the mentalistic concepts inherited from British empiricism.

The major division of learning theory is the outcome of disagreements between the original behaviorists and the Gestalt psychologists. The neobehaviorists, as they are frequently called, believe that learning is best treated as stimulus-response relationships. They are divided themselves, however, over the issue of reinforcement as a necessary condition of learning. One group of neobehaviorists believes that the attachment or linkage of a given response to a specified stimulus is contingent upon some kind of reinforcement, either in the form of drive reduction, need gratification, confirmation of expectations, or simply "effect." The other group contends that a stimulus and response need only be contiguous; if a response follows a specified stimulus, then that particular response becomes associated with the stimulus. The primary issue with S-R theory, therefore, is one of reinforcement versus contiguity.

The cognitive or field theorists are skeptical of the neobehaviorist's efforts to isolate stimulus variables and establish S-R relations. As the inheritors of Gestalt principles, the cognitive theorists regard the pattern of organization of the stimulus variables as crucial. Perceptual processes are regarded as the factors necessary to explain learned behavior, and the subject's "psychological field" rather than the physical stimuli is regarded as the proper focal point of the psychologist's attention. How the subject perceives the situation is more important than the physical dimensions of the stimulating variables.

If the neobehaviorists and cognitive theorists may be regarded as a second generation of behaviorists and Gestaltists, there is a third group of psychologists whose work in learning continues the tradition established by Ebbinghaus. This group of psychologists do not call themselves functionalists but their approach to learning displays the same flexibility and accommodating attitude that the early functionalists showed. More concerned with establishing empirical facts than constructing theories and systems of learning, these psychologists have remained apart from the theoretical issues debated by the cognitive theorists and neobehaviorists. Whereas the latter have shown a preference for experimentation with animals, the contemporary functionalists have been primarily interested in human verbal learning, and they have continued to exploit the many advantages of nonsense syllables. They have provided a great deal of empirical knowledge which is not dependent upon theory for interpretation.

THEORIES OF PERCEPTION

If learning research and theory have absorbed the major attention of American psychologists in the past thirty years, it may be that research and theory in perception command the spotlight at present. Technological innovations in the field of electronics have provided instrumentation permitting investigations of the neurophysiology of sensation that would have been impossible twenty years ago. The result has been "a renaissance of sensory psychology." Indeed, it would not be improper to speculate that more ingenious research is currently being conducted in the field of sensation and perception than any other area of contemporary psychology.

Research and theory in perception have been influenced greatly by Gestalt psychology, and convergence with methodological behaviorism is evident, but the spirit of current research is definitely functionalistic. Instead of investigating the properties of physical stimuli and their effect upon perceptual response, as in traditional or classical psychophysics, an increasing number of psychologists are studying the effect of organismic variables upon perception. This shift of emphasis has resulted in numerous experiments relating perception to such variables as motives, opinions, beliefs, needs, anxiety, attitudes, and values. Other studies have probed more deeply into personality characteristics in an effort to determine the relations between perception of the exterior world and "ongoing processes" within the subjects.

At least one current issue in perception theory, however, is a vestige of the nineteenth century. Perceptual theorists are still divided over the issue of nativism versus empiricism. Numerous studies conducted by psychologists of behavioristic bent underscore the role of previous experience in perception and emphasize learning as the major determinant. Other studies by contemporary functionalists demonstrate that perception is instrumental to our efforts to adapt or adjust to the world around us. The defense of inherent organizing factors, as claimed by the Gestalt psychologists, continues, nonetheless, and the issue of nativism versus empiricism will remain for years to come.

Perhaps no recent theory in psychology has stimulated as much interest as the "directive state theories" of perception. Frequently referred to as "the new look in psychology," these experiments dealing with "interior" constructs such as motives and emotions as perceptual determinants have not only produced empirical findings of high interest but triggered considerable theorizing concerning perceptual processes as a basis for a comprehensive behavior theory. If one mark of a theory's effectiveness is its stimulation of research, then the "directive state theories" of perception may be regarded as one of the "better" psychological theories to appear in recent years.

THEORIES OF PERSONALITY

Catching the attention of psychologists later than the topics of learning and perception, theories of motivation are not as systematically developed as theories in the other two areas. Since, however, motivational processes are the crux of most personality theories, we may briefly consider the numerous efforts to construct theories and systems of personality.

Personality theorists have aimed for a higher degree of integration and comprehensiveness than the learning or perceptual theorists, and much of the respect commanded by personality theories stems directly from their treatment of variables that psychologists working in perception and learning have been unwilling to consider. Most current theories of personality reflect the influence of Freudian psychology in their concern with unconscious determinants of behavior, the importance attributed to early experiences in infancy and childhood, and the focus of attention on development and adjustment. While recognizing the role of unconscious determinants, however, personality theorists vary greatly in the emphasis placed on unconscious motives as opposed to "conscious intent" and capacity variables.

It is in the realm of motivation or personality that psychological theory has received both the most publicity and the most serious criticisms. Many of the criticisms are aimed at psychoanalytic concepts and principles that were not only modified by Freud himself in later years but have been altered further by a group of his followers known as neoanalysts. Because psychoanalysis is both a theory of personality and a method of psychological treatment, it has been especially easy for critics to confuse the two.

Despite the apparent lack of empirical substance of many personality theories, we may speculate that efforts to validate experimentally the insights of personality theorists will be intensified in future years. Many of the concepts and principles of personality theory are proving amenable to experimentation and analysis within the framework of stimulus-response theory, and until better empirical footing is gained, the diversity of theories may be regarded as a source of strength rather than weakness.

MINIATURE THEORIES AND MODELS

Several of the theories referred to in discussing theories of learning and perception are sometimes called miniature theories. This implies that the theory has been developed to account for a specific segment of behavior, such as rote memory, problem solving, decision making, social motivation, or the neurophysiology of motivation. Because of the advantage of limiting research to a specific set of problems, the construction of miniature theories and models has become exceedingly popular in the past twenty years. The objective is to delineate closely an area of work and then to devise the simplest theory or model capable of handling the empirical concepts and relationships in the area. As more data are acquired and as more complex problems are encountered, the theory or model is enlarged in order to accommodate the additional knowledge.

The construction of models in psychology has been spurred by the innovations of cybernetics and information or communication theory. Electronic or mechanical models are constructed *as if* similar psychological processes could be explained by comparable mechanisms. Indeed, many of the servo-mechanisms based on the feedback principle are quite "animal-like" in their operations, but it is well to remember that the models are descriptive of psychological processes and relations rather than explanatory; animal behavior is not explained by the functional similarity with mechanical or electrical models. Model construction can be highly effective by (1) lending precision and accuracy to our predictions, (2) suggesting ways in which intervening variables might operate, (3) sharpening or clarifying our understanding of psychological processes, and (4) suggesting better methods of investigating the events mediating stimulus and response.

Some psychologists believe that the application of engineering concepts and principles to the study of psychological problems will be highly accelerated in coming years. The increasing concern with data-processing devices has stimulated research in comparable psychological processes, and as more complex computers are designed, we will gain better insight into human thought and decision making. The functional similarity between neurological systems and computer systems is striking, to say the least, and there can be no doubt that computers will play an extensive role in future psychological research.

Methods
of Inquiry

During the debate among schools, psychology was seriously hampered by the uncritical acceptance of theory as facts. Both theory and fact are essential to science, but it is always well to distinguish between the two. As we have seen, the schools of psychology continued to argue theory long after they were silent about each other's empirical facts.

It is frequently said, in support of theory, that the mere accumulation and cataloguing of facts is meaningless without some framework into which they can be incorporated. It is also said that theory without empirical data is mere speculation. Both points of view are correct and, fortunately for psychology, we need not choose between them. The acquisition of empirical facts and the systematizing of those facts are complementary processes; one without the other gives us an incomplete achievement. Not only does theory influence choice of method but method influences both theory and empirical findings. There is much to be said, therefore, in favor of beginning with methods and proceeding to theory. Indeed, there is good reason to believe that the methods by which empirical data are gathered can provide the most meaningful background against which to view contemporary psychology.

Methods of psychological inquiry are customarily referred to as experimental, statistical, and clinical. In recent years there has been an increasing rapprochement among the three methods so that they should no longer be regarded as separate and distinct. Almost all experimental methods now involve some kind of statistical analysis; the same is true of clinical methods. Moreover, there is an increasing tendency to combine clinical and experimental methods so that the common ground between the three methods is expanding. Yet, each of the three methods has its distinctive features and these are what we shall emphasize here. A brief description of each method is given below and a succeeding chapter is devoted to a more complete discussion of each.

EXPERIMENTAL METHODS

We have seen that experimentation in science is planned and controlled observation. There is no longer any debate as to whether psychology is an experimental science or not. The work of Ebbinghaus in the nineteenth century demonstrated the applicability of experimental techniques to "the higher mental processes." Still many critics of experimentation in psychology express the belief that the work of experimental psychologists is trivial, that it does not come to grips with important behavior, that it concerns itself exclusively with superficial behavior.

The criticism of experimental methods in psychology may stem from the confusion of experimental psychology with laboratory psychology. As we shall see, the two are not synonymous. Experimental methods are applied to problems outside the laboratory as well as those within. We must admit, however, that better forms of control are permissible within the laboratory setting. Far from being the artificial setting it is sometimes supposed to be, the psychological laboratory is the most productive source of psychological facts.

STATISTICAL METHODS

The extensive use of quantitative techniques in psychology often comes as a surprise to beginning students. Living close to a common sense definition of psychology, they do not anticipate a need for mathematics as a research tool. But a mark of progress in science is the use of measurement and here psychology may boast that not only has it made impressive progress but it has developed techniques which have been borrowed by other sciences; even physicists have been known to use some of the psychophysical methods developed by psychologists.

Statistical methods may be regarded as including all applications of quantitative techniques to psychological problems. Not all psychologists will agree with such a classification, but it may be justified in the interest of economy. Statistical methods are sometimes said to be employed where experimentation is less practical.

Experimental principles may be employed, however as in the control of experimental variables through the selection of subjects and the use of control groups. It is not quite fair, therefore, to place statistical methods in the position of "second best"; a better distinction would be in terms of the different kinds of problems that each is best equipped to handle.

CLINICAL METHODS

The use of clinical methods was seen previously in our discussion of Broca's discovery of the speech area. Broca's approach was opportunistic in that he took advantage of a situation already created to make his observations. It's a bit poetic to speak of the clinical method as a capitalization on nature's experiments, but there is some truth in the statement. There are many occasions in life whereby the psychologist may observe ongoing events which he did nothing to produce but for which he is grateful for the opportunity to observe. Such occasions would be the events of war, the actions of a lynch mob, a crime of passion, a psychotic episode, an emotional disturbance, and a May Day festival.

Here we are placing clinical methods within the framework of natural observation but we shall not leave them there. As clinical methods have been developed, they have relied more and more on specialized techniques and procedures. These have been developed to observe more subtle aspects of behavior and to handle a different level of problems, providing us with all the more reason for discussing separately in more detail the three methods of inquiry we have introduced.

The Experimental
Approach in
Psychology 5

Experimental success in investigating psychological problems is limited by only two factors—the psychologist's ingenuity and his ethics. Given the ground rules of experimental research, the psychologist is thrown upon his own resources to overcome the numerous handicaps he will encounter in studying human behavior; his success in doing so will be a direct function of his ability to move around, under, and over the barriers without distorting his experimental findings in the process. But because his experimental subjects are so often members of the human race, the psychologist cannot exceed the proprieties of society or the dictates of respect for human welfare. In other words, he cannot abuse his subjects or resort to methods of deceit which will humiliate or insult his subjects. Nor may he employ techniques which endanger the lives of his subjects or leave harmful aftereffects when the experiment is concluded.

Objectives and
General Procedures

In essence, the objective of the psychologist in the experimental situation is the objective of all experimental scientists. The psychologist seeks to establish functional relationships between specified variables by ordering or arranging suitable conditions for observation; in doing so, his first task is to identify, isolate, and control the relevant variables in the situation.

As we have seen, the classic model of experimental research in which the experimenter deals with a single independent variable and a single dependent variable is difficult to achieve. The number of variables which may be operating in a given situation are often numerous and the psychologist is especially hardput to control all variables in a situation as complex as a psychological experiment. Fortunately, it is not necessary for him to control them all; it is merely necessary for him to identify and control the variables which are relevant to the behavior he would observe and record. For example, in a verbal learning experiment the color of the subjects' eyes may well be a variable but it is extremely doubtful that it is a relevant one. The same would not be true, however, of individual differences in the subjects' abilities to deal with abstract symbols and relations. Intelligence is a variable logically expected to influence performance on a learning task, and in any learning experiment, the psychologist would do well to exercise some control over the intelligence of his subjects. That is to say, he must be able to discount the likelihood that individual differences in intelligence alone are responsible for the subjects' performance during the experiment.

The identification of relevant variables, therefore, is definitely related to the psychologist's sophistication in his particular area of research. It is assumed that he has familiarized himself with the studies made previously by others and that he will exercise due sensitivity to the operation of subtle or indirect variables which may influence his observations. No one should expect the psychologist to be omniscient about such matters, but by and large we expect him to point a finger at variables which could account for the results of his experiment.

Having identified the relevant variables in his experimental situation, the psychologist is then confronted with the problem of isolating them so that they may be manipulated or controlled. The fact that relevant variables are often related not only to the dependent variable but to each other makes the problem of isolation quite difficult in many experiments. For example, socioeconomic class is a variable affecting the behavior of subjects in many experimental situations. Yet, socioeconomic class is a highly complex variable in itself and identification of socioeconomic class as a variable does not tell us whether we are talking about family income, home and community environment, father's occupation, cultural background, or a combination of the many other variables that are so frequently lumped together as socioeconomic class.

If, in a particular experiment, a psychologist regarded socioeconomic class as a relevant variable and desired to rule out its influence upon the behavior of his subjects, it would be necessary for him to tell us what he means by socioeconomic class. The problem of isolating variables is obviously related, therefore, to the problem of operational definitions. How the psychologist identifies and isolates the variable of socioeconomic class will depend directly on how he defines the concept. The more specific and the more concrete his definition, the more likely he will be able to control or assess the influence of such a variable upon the performance of his subjects.

In an experiment studying the relationship between the motivation of children and their judgment of the monetary value of various objects, the psychologist may hold socioeconomic class constant by selecting groups of children on the basis of reported family income, father's occupation, or place of residence. The psychologist would attempt to rule out the effect of a disturbing variable by equating his experimental groups with respect to that particular variable. It is obvious in this particular example that the psychologist has not controlled each and every one of the many variables making up socioeconomic class; the point is, however, that he has told us what he means by use of the concept, and he has taken steps to control its influence upon his dependent variable.

Experimental and Behavioral Variables

The problems of identifying, isolating, and controlling the operative variables in an experiment may be better understood by consideration of the types of variables involved. We have mentioned that traditionally the variables in experimentation are referred to as the independent variables and the dependent variables. Intentionally or not, the classical experimental design implies that the experimenter must hold constant all variables except one. This single variable is designated the independent variable and the scientist causes it to vary systematically while he observes the effect of its variation upon the dependent variable, the phenomenon he is trying to understand and explain. This description of scientific method has the advantage of simplicity, but it describes research as it is seldom conducted.

For psychology it makes more sense to speak of two classes of variables in an experiment. One class, the behavioral variables, are those dimensions, attributes, or features of the subjects' behavior that the psychologist has chosen to study; the other class, the experimental variables, are those that he seeks to control or manipulate and thereby relate to the behavioral variables.

The behavioral variables in a psychological experiment are obviously those commonly referred to as dependent variables. The plural is used in discussing them here because so often we find that the psychologist has not limited himself to a single aspect of behavior, but is seeking to understand several aspects. In other words, the behavioral variables are the consequences of the experiment which the psychologist will seek to explain in terms of the antecedent experimental variables. They are the criteria of his experiment and his job is to predict or explain them from the experimental variables.

The problem of identifying, isolating, and defining the behavioral variables are identical with those of the experimental variables. The behavioral variables, after all, are highly relevant to the success of the experiment and, as often comes as a surprise to the beginning psychology student, they are by no means given; the psychologist must ferret them out.

Despite much glib talk about "observing the subjects' behavior" we don't really mean that we merely look on while the subjects go through their paces. We can observe intelligently only when we are set to look for some specific aspect of the subjects' behavior. To observe and record the total sum of the subjects' behavior in even the simplest experimental situation would require a prohibitive outlay of equipment. It would require a movie camera to record body movements, a tape recorder to record speech, a polygraph to detect physiological changes, and still we would miss most of what was going on. The psychologist will seldom resort to such extravagance because his research budget will not permit it; even in a Utopia where money was plentiful, the expenditure would be unnecessary because all dimensions of behavior are not equally relevant in a given situation. While participating in an experiment, most experimental subjects are usually digesting their most recent meal but the psychologist is seldom interested in this aspect of their behavior.

The psychologist must isolate, therefore, those aspects of behavior which are relevant to his inquiry. The work of psychological research must be divided and he must leave to others the problem of explaining other aspects of the subjects' behavior. His choice of a criterion is a crucial one. It must be specific, concrete, and pertinent.

Actually, there are very few experiments in which the psychologist merely observes the subjects' behavior. More often, he will seek to record or measure the behavior in which he is interested. This permits a more permanent record of what transpired in the experiment and makes the psychologist's behavioral variables more concrete. In most psychological experiments, the behavioral variables are not so much behavior as they are products of behavior. The subjects are asked to record their own responses in such a way as to provide the psychologist a permanent and quantifiable record for analysis and interpretation.

The gist, then, is that rather than recording the response itself, the psychologist will endeavor to observe and record such features as the accuracy of the response, its speed, its strength, and the proportion of correct responses given in a certain period of time or on a certain number of trials. Occasionally he will rely on a subjective report or try to devise measures of the physical energy expended by the subject in making the response. The kind of behavioral variables used by the psychologist may be illustrated best by a sampling of dependent variables used in laboratory learning experiments: (1) amplitude of response, as in a galvanic skin response, (2) latency of response, as in the time taken to escape from a puzzlebox, (3) rate of response, as in the number of times a rat presses a bar in a given period of time, (4) speed of response, as in the time taken by a rat to run a maze, (5) number of trials, as taken by the subject to memorize a list of nonsense syllables, (6) total time, as taken to solve a difficult puzzle, (7) direction of movement, as used in avoidance learning, (8) number of trials required to extinguish a response, as in conditioning experiments, and (9) detection, number, and quality of errors, as used in learning certain types of verbal materials.

Classes of Experimental Variables

The experimental variables dealt with by psychologists in experimental research may be classified into four different types: (1) subject, (2) situational, (3) treatment, and (4) task variables.

Subject variables in psychological experiments are the individual differences of the subjects. These are the characteristics of the individuals who participate in the experiment as opposed to the characteristics of the situation. Typical examples of subject variables are age, sex, intellectual capacities, education, occupation, socioeconomic status, cultural background, national origin, motivation, attitudes, opinions, beliefs, and physical features. The relevance of such variables depends directly upon the nature of the situation, treatment, and task variables. If any of these are subject to influence by the individual differences of the subjects, then steps must be taken by the psychologist to control the bias that might enter his findings. The influence of subject variables is often subtle and may limit severely the extent to which the psychologist may generalize his results.

Situational variables pertain to the physical equipment, facilities, and conditions of the experiment. These may include environmental factors such as temperature, humidity, illumination, and ventilation, but would also include social factors such as size of group, personal characteristics of group members, and even the personality of the psychologist.

Treatment variables may be identified as anything or everything the psychologist does to the subject during the experiment. These would include the instructions given the subjects, the conditions under which they perform the experimental task, the way in which materials are presented for learning, the practice conditions specified by the psychologist, the knowledge of results given the subjects, the quality, type, and frequency of reinforcement, and the rate at which the subjects are required to perform. They also might include more direct forms of manipulation by the psychologist, such as the administration of drugs, the requirement that the subjects undergo long periods of deprivation, or the prolongation of stress or fatigue. In the case of animals, the intervention of the psychologist may be even more drastic, such as extirpation of cortical regions, the implantation of electrodes in the subcortical regions of the brain, or subjection to excessive stress or fatigue.

Task variables are the features or characteristics of the task or apparatus confronting the subjects. This class of variables would include the nature of the task itself, its magnitude and complexity, and its similarity to previous tasks performed by the same subjects. Although related to subject variables, such factors as meaningfulness of the task, interest to subjects, and affectivity should be included in this class of variables because they are more easily controlled if treated as properties of the task than as personal characteristics of the subjects.

The Control of
Experimental Variables

If the essence of experimental method in science is the control of relevant variables, the psychologist's success as an experimental scientist is dependent upon his ability to manipulate his experimental variables. His methods of control are seldom direct, but they must have the effect of isolating the relevant variables and permitting the psychologist to assess their influence on his dependent behavioral variables. Manipulation of experimental variables by the psychologist does not involve the same degree of precision and accuracy that the physicist enjoys, but manipulation is more often possible in psychological research than commonly supposed.

SUBJECT VARIABLES

The control of subject variables is the most frequently criticized aspect of psychological experiments. In a society that gives much lip service to the desirability of individual differences, the layman finds it difficult to believe that the psychologist's research findings are not peculiar to the subjects he used. When individual differences of experimental subjects are known to be relevant to the experimental setting, the psychologist must, of course, make adjustment for them. If his research findings cannot be generalized beyond his subjects, the usefulness of the findings is extremely limited.

When two or more treatments are involved in an experiment, the most obvious way of controlling subject variables is to use the same subjects in all treatments. By employing the same individuals in all experimental treatments, individual differences would supposedly be constant from treatment to treatment. The only problem with this form of control is the fact that the behavior of a single individual varies from situation to situation. Because of such disturbing factors as learning, fatigue, loss of interest, or unsustained attention, we can never expect the individual's behavior to remain constant for all experimental treatments. In short, the psychologist can never expect his subjects to perform equally well on all experimental tasks or under all experimental treatments.

When a subject variable itself is the independent variable in an experiment, it is impossible to use the subjects as their own control because the variable is so seldom subject to manipulation. For example, the psychologist might be trying to determine if Baptists or Methodists make better astronauts but he could not orbit an astronaut once as a Baptist and then again as a Methodist; his influence over church membership is too limited.

Another fairly obvious way of controlling subject variables is to match subjects who will perform on the different experimental tasks or participate in the different experimental treatments. This method has been used frequently in psychological research but rarely in a satisfactory manner. Not only are there difficulties in specifying exactly which subject variables should be used to match subjects, but there are almost unsurmountable difficulties involved in obtaining two groups of comparable subjects. One of the few occasions on which this type of control is effective is when the subjects are sets of identical twins.

Better control of subject variables may be gained by matching groups rather than sets of individual subjects. The matching of experimental groups becomes quite elaborate when we deal with several subject variables at different levels. This may involve the use of stratified samples, a method of grouping subjects in such a way that a certain percent of each experimental group will have a given characteristic. In studying the influence of education upon the perception or judgment of people, for example, we may deliberately draw our subjects for each experimental task in such a way that we get an equal proportion of subjects at specified educational levels.

In recent years psychologists have resorted more and more to the control of subject variables through a process known as randomization, a procedure involving the selection of a total group of subjects and their random assignment to the experimental tasks or treatments. By random assignment we mean, of course, that any particular subject has the same possibility of being assigned to each of the experimental treatments and that all experimental subjects have the same likelihood of being assigned to a particular experimental treatment.

Randomization as a method of controlling subject variables

makes more sense when we recognize that almost always in experimental research we are interested in observed differences between two or more groups of subjects. It is not the absolute performance of a group on a given task or under a given treatment that concerns us but rather the performance of that particular group in reference to other groups of known variation. If we are able to assume that the experimental groups differ only in the characteristic we have designated as the independent variable, then we are justified in attributing the observed difference in experimental group performance to the influence of that characteristic. The assumption that the experimental groups do not differ significantly in subject variables is best warranted when subjects have been assigned to the tasks or treatments in random order.

The whys and wherefores of randomization are too complex to explain in short order, but we may see something of its importance in an experimental situation involving two simple treatments. Given a group of twenty experimental subjects, we would not permit the individual subject to choose the experimental treatment he would undergo because his reasons for choosing a particular treatment would introduce a source of error we could not control. Unknown to us, one of the experimental treatments might appear more pleasant to the subjects or they might think it would take less time. By permitting the subjects to choose the experimental treatment, we would introduce the variable of individual preference to confound any differences we might observe between the two treatment groups. Individual preference, as well as other subject variables, would be randomized if we assigned subjects to the different treatments by a flip of a coin or by drawing their names out of a hat.

SITUATIONAL VARIABLES

The control of situational variables in psychological research can be achieved only by standardization of the situation under which the subjects are studied. If a situational variable is to be the independent variable in the experiment, then rigorous care must be taken to rule out the effect of other variables which may be operative in the situation. To study the effect of a situational variable such as illumination upon a behavioral variable such as job performance, we would be required to control the influence of other variables such as ventilation, humidity, temperature, and other working conditions. Adequate control of such variables would require a high degree of standardization; any condition which conceivably would affect the behavioral variable would need to be identified and its effect isolated.

The removal of our subjects to a laboratory setting would permit better control of many types of situational variables but such action might introduce another source of error in the form of suggestion or improved motivation of subjects. Since any psychological experiment is a matter of give-and-take, the experimenter must decide if the advantages of controlling situational variables in a laboratory setting are great enough to offset the disadvantages of spurious subject variables. In most laboratory experiments, it would appear that the more rigorous control of situational variables is highly desirable.

When subject, task, or treatment variables are the independent variables in an experiment, the influence of situational variables may be quite subtle. The difficulty of identifying situational variables which affect the behavioral variables is appreciable when the situations vary greatly for different groups of subjects. To some extent it is possible to randomize the effect of such variables, but frequently the psychologist is forced to assume random effect without being able to take steps to assure it.

TREATMENT VARIABLES

When treatments are the independent variables in a psychological experiment, great care must be taken to assure that the treatments do not differ in unintended respects. The treatments must be uniform for all subjects within a given treatment group and the treatments must not differ in any way which is not predetermined by the psychologist. The necessity of uniformity within treatment groups is best illustrated by the use of placebos in experiments involving the administration of drugs. Because the administration of any drug carries considerable suggestion, it is necessary to give a "sugar-coated" pill to a control group which is comparable to the experimental group receiving the more potent drug. A test of the drug's effect upon the behavioral variables requires, therefore, at least two control groups—one that receives no drug of any kind and one that receives a drug which is impotent. This is the only way in which the effect of suggestion can be controlled.

Although not as obvious or dramatic as experiments involving drugs, the effects of suggestion can be quite pronounced in other experiments where treatment variables are manipulated. The manner in which subjects perceive the experimental treatment or the response they make to the differential treatment may produce a spurious effect in their performance. The psychologist cannot assume easily that two or more experimental treatments differ in one respect only; often they differ in ways unsuspected by the experimenter.

TASK VARIABLES

When subjects are asked to serve on two or more experimental tasks, sequential effects such as practice or fatigue are often controlled by a method known as counterbalancing. This method involves the presentation of different orders of tasks to different groups of subjects. For example, one group may proceed from Task A to Task B while a comparable group proceeds from Task B to Task A. Any effect of the first task upon the second will thereby be nullified when the scores or performance indices on Task A are combined for analysis.

Counterbalancing is one of the oldest and simplest means of controlling serial effects in psychological research. It rests on an assumption, however, that any transfer or carry-over from Task A to Task B is the same as that from Task B to Task A. If the psychologist has not constructed his two tasks carefully, it might turn out that the assumption is unwarranted. There may be something built into Task A which facilitates performance on Task B but not vice versa. For this reason counterbalancing as a means of control is used less and less in psychological research.

Task variables in psychological experiments are especially susceptible to error from irrelevant or transitory sources. The task may be constructed in such a manner as to be invalid for purposes of the experiment. Unless the psychologist has pretested his task, he cannot be certain that it requires the specific form of behavior that he desires. The same would be true of the task's reliability. The psychologist must determine in advance that the task will provide stable, consistent measures of the subject's performance. If the task gives results which are actually irrelevant to the experiment or if it fails to give consistent results over a period of time, the psychologist is unable to use the task as part of his experimental inquiry.

Experimental Design
and Statistical Analysis

It is evident from the previous discussion that psychological experimentation is a means of comparing the performance of two or more groups when the groups are (1) composed of subjects with different characteristics, (2) subjected to differential treatment, (3) presented with different tasks, or (4) placed in different situations. Because of inherent variation in each of the four classes of experimental variables, the psychologist must take rigorous steps to assure that the observed variation in the performance of his subjects is a function of his independent variable rather than variation from other sources. Unless he has ruled out the effects of extraneous or uncontrolled variables in his experiment, he cannot attribute the observed performance of his subjects to the operation of his independent variable.

To assess the extent of sampling error in the observed results, some form of statistical analysis is involved in virtually all psychological experiments. Because the difference in performance between the experimental groups may be a chance variation itself, some form of statistical test is conducted to eliminate the likelihood that the observed difference is *nothing but* a chance variation.

The convergence of experimental and statistical methods has produced methods of research that are a far cry from the classic design of a single independent variable and its functional effect upon a dependent variable. The development of multivariate experimental designs now permits the simultaneous consideration of several experimental variables in psychological research, gaining advantages of both economy and precision. Not only may the psychologist study the effect of the separate experimental variables on the performance of his subjects but he may study the effect of the experimental variables operating in conjunction with each other. Indeed, the interaction effects, as they are known, of two or more experimental variables operating concurrently may be more significant than the effect of any one variable considered individually. For example, the psychologist may study the effect of two or more subject variables upon the behavior of his subjects; or the effect of a subject variable operating in conjunction with a situational, task, or treatment variable; or the effect of subject, situational, task, and treatment variables operating concurrently in any conceivable combination. Each of the experimental variables may be varied systematically and its effect upon the subjects' behavior partialed out for separate study.

The concept of interaction is not easy to explain. In effect, it implies that the outcome of two simultaneous events is greater than or less than the same two events occurring successively. The outcome is not a cumulative or additive effect of the two events, and by occurring simultaneously the two events either increase or diminish the expected results. Another way of explaining interaction is to say that the relationship between two variables is dependent upon intrinsic characteristics of the two variables or interplay with a third variable. An example of interaction may be given by numerous recent studies of the relationship between motivation and performance. Almost invariably, these studies demonstrate that the relationship between degree of motivation and quality of performance is dependent upon the difficulty or complexity of the task. That is to say, for a given level of difficulty in the task, an increase in motivation results in an increase in performance. If, however, the task becomes "too difficult," further increase in motivation results in a decline in performance.

Other examples of interaction may be given by studies relating the effectiveness of leadership to situational variables such as the size of a group, its organization, or its cohesiveness. Certain personal characteristics of the leader or certain behavior on his part may be quite effective for groups of a certain size and organization. Again, however, if the group becomes "too large" or "reorganized," the previous leadership exercised may become completely ineffective.

Many other examples of interaction among psychological variables could be given, but the important point is that multivariate designs permit the psychologist not only to study several experimental variables at a time but also to study the combined effects of the variables. Often the effect of two or more variables operating conjointly will produce an effect upon performance, whereas, each operating separately has no significant effect.

The statistical rationale for analyzing the results of a multivariate design is one of accounting for the variation of the subjects' performance in terms of the experimental variables selected for study. By using a set of statistical techniques known as analysis of variance, the psychologist is able to break down the variation in performance which is due to each of the experimental variables; the outcome of the analysis is the same as if he had conducted several experiments simultaneously.

The use of multivariate designs and analysis of variance techniques in psychology illustrate the inseparable ties between experimental and statistical methods. Although complex in appearance, they are highly economical in the sense of giving maximum information for the number of subjects used and the number of variables manipulated. They have the added advantage of bringing the experimental situation "closer to reality" because the complexity of the variables and their interaction more closely approaches what we observe in "real life."

The Statistical
Approach in
Psychology   6

Measurement techniques in psychology have developed along two independent lines. One line of development has maintained the traditions of psychophysical methods which have remained tools of the trade for experimental psychologists. The other line stems from man's gambling proclivities and a healthy concern of British and American psychologists with individual differences.

Although statistical methods are said to originate in speculation about games of chance, gamblers had intuitive laws of probability long before mathematicians established the mathematical basis for such laws. It was not until the eighteenth century that de Moivre derived the normal distribution curve and it was the nineteenth century before Laplace published his work on probability. De Moivre's normal distribution curve was shown by Gauss to depict with practical accuracy both the measurements and errors made by scientists, and Quetelet (1796-1874), a Belgian astronomer, applied the normal curve to biological and social data. Quetelet's work was the beginning of statistics as the field is now known. He demonstrated that physical measurements of people were distributed in accordance with the law of normal distribution, and he made the interesting speculation that nature had tried to produce an ideal average man but fell short of its target on many individuals. "Quetelet's law," if it may be so honored, was the first attempt to interpret human characteristics in terms of deviation from a statistical norm.

In England Sir Francis Galton took note of Quetelet's work and set up his anthropological laboratory at South Kensington to study the over-all problem of human variation. Galton found that the normal curve was an inadequate description of the distribution of many characteristics but his work may be regarded as the beginning of the testing movement in psychology.

James McKeen Cattell (1860-1944), an American student of Wundt's at the University of Leipzig, became interested in Galton's work and upon his return to America undertook the study of individual differences with the kind of sensory, motor, and perceptual tests that Galton had devised in his laboratory. Cattell's efforts employed a combination of experimental methods and mental testing. Conducting experiments on reaction time, attention span, and controlled association, Cattell also developed tests of sensory acuity, motor capacities, and perceptual skills for administration to college students. Few of Cattell's tests proved to be of value in predicting performance in college, but his work, more than anyone else's, spurred the study of individual differences in America.

The influence of Galton's and Cattell's work on the subsequent development of psychology was pronounced because of the techniques and methods they introduced. Galton not only applied the normal probability curve to individual differences but devised a number of statistical techniques which are still widely used today. In addition to contributing the term "mental test" to the vocabulary of psychology, Cattell provided concepts of psychological testing which were reformed by later workers to become a distinctive characteristic of American psychology as opposed to European brands.

Despite the fact that the relationship between psychophysics and mental testing is quite strong and despite the fact that both lines of development were influenced by Cattell, the two developments remained apart for most of their formative years. Psychophysical techniques were employed by experimental psychologists who took little notice of the development in psychological testing, while the psychologists interested in test construction missed many of the applications they might have made of psychophysical methods. The experimental psychologists concerned themselves exclusively with the uniformities or regularities of behavior and regarded individual differences as something of a nuisance to be endured. The bridge was eventually built by the psychometricians who began to rationalize their testing methods with psychophysical theory as the basis.

The Nature of
Statistical Thought

The concept of variation is crucial to both statistical methods and a science of behavior. Not only do organisms differ from each other but the individual organism's behavior varies from situation to situation. Because our observations of the organism's behavior cannot be continuous, what we observe in a given situation will necessarily depend upon the situation and the time chosen to observe. This implies that what we observe is subject to error because our observations may not be representative of all situations and all conditions within which our subjects behave. The experimental psychologist counteracts this type of sampling error by specifying carefully the conditions under which he observes the behavior of his subjects, but his observations are still subject to sampling error.

Sampling error is implicit in all that the psychologist does. In any set of observations or measurements, the psychologist must regard his data as a sample drawn from a larger population of possible observations. Indeed, the essence of statistical methods may be regarded as a means of drawing conclusions about a larger class of events from a subset of those events. Virtually never in science do we deal with the entire population of events and entities in which we are interested but rather a sample of that population. From the sample we draw conclusions concerning the total class of events, recognizing in doing so, that our conclusions are subject to some degree of sampling error. Where characteristics of a species are relatively constant, as in the physical features of certain animals, sampling error may be so negligible as to be disregarded. But in characteristics of high variability, such as the behavior of 6-year-old children, sampling error may be extremely large.

A fundamental problem confronting every psychologist, then, is the determination of sampling error in his observations. If sampling error is large, he can generalize his findings only if he is willing to run great risks of being wrong; if sampling error is small, both he and others can put better confidence in the psychologist's research findings. Since the ultimate objective of research is to extend or generalize its findings, the validity or usefulness of the psychologist's observations is a direct function of the sampling error involved.

Sampling error in psychology may be defined as the probability that the observations made in a particular research study are peculiar to the subjects and tasks employed in the study. If the probability is quite high, then generalization of the research findings to other situations and other subjects may not be warranted. The probability that the outcome of a research study is due to sampling error alone is inversely related to the confidence one can put in the conclusion; the less the probability that sampling error is responsible for the outcome, the more confidence we can have in our findings.

Probability may be regarded best as the frequency with which we expect events to occur. This means simply that we have some notion of how frequently we expect certain events to occur and we compare the event observed in our research with the expected frequency of occurrence to determine its statistical significance. The frequency with which we expect events to occur may be intuitive, rational, or empirical.

Intuitive probability is used by virtually everyone in making sundry decisions. In many cases it may be no more than a subjective feeling of certainty or doubt. We say that despite a poor home environment a child will probably turn out to be a respectable citizen or that a friend would like to be president of an organization but he probably won't be elected. In either case our statement is an expression of doubt or confidence concerning the outcome of some future event. Occasionally we try to be more sophisticated and declare that the odds are two to one that an invited guest will not come or that chances are 95 in 100 that he will not bring his wife with him, but our notion of probability is still intuitive. We have neither a rational nor an empirical basis for stating the expected outcome in terms of odds or chances.

A rational basis for probability is provided when we can state the probability of an event as its ratio to the total number of possible events. This implies that all possible events in a given situation are equally likely to occur and a specific event has the same opportunity as any other. The inevitable example of this kind of probability is the ubiquitous six-sided die in which the probability of rolling any particular number is one out of six. Our notions of probability here are applicable only if we can assume that the die is an honest one and that it will be rolled in a fair manner. Other forms of rational or a priori probability are seen in the binomial expansion so greatly suffered by algebra students and in the normal probability curve discussed previously.

An empirical basis for probability is given by the relative frequency of specifically defined events. This implies that the events have actually been observed by someone and a tabulation of relative frequency made. We are all familiar with this type of probability through statistics of automobile accidents provided by the National Safety Council or similar statistics on the number of persons struck by lightning or those killed in airplane crashes. Most of us conclude from these statistics that the probability of our own death at the hands of a car, plane, or thunderbolt is quite low because of the relatively low frequency with which others are so killed.

Our notions of intuitive, rational, and empirical probability are not unrelated to each other but it is well to recognize the operation of all three in scientific work. Most scientists prefer empirical concepts of probability when possible, but rational principles of probability play an important role in the testing of scientific hypotheses, and no little scientific research has been known to begin with intuitive notions of probability. The isomorphism, if we may borrow a term from the Gestalt psychologists, of rational and empirical notions of probability may be seen in the close approximation of the distribution of many empirical events to the normal probability curve. The distribution of errors of measurement and errors of estimation definitely appear to be in keeping with the normal curve.

As mentioned previously, many physical, biological, and psychological measurements have been observed to approximate the normal curve in large, unselected populations. The result of this happy coincidence is that the normal probability curve has proven to be one of the psychologist's most useful conceptional tools.

Purposes of Statistics

Statistical methods serve many purposes in psychology. The purposes served are not peculiar to psychology, however, but may be regarded as those of all sciences. The major purposes of statistical methods are identified as (1) simplification of complex data, (2) description of group characteristics, (3) comparison of groups, and (4) quantification of relationships.

SIMPLIFYING DATA

All sciences are said to begin with the collection, arranging, ordering, and classifying of facts. The data of science quickly achieve a complexity which would be overwhelming without some means of simplifying or organizing them. When the data involve quantities which have been counted or measured, the methods of classification employed are statistical. The necessity of classification arises from the fact that numerical data must be arranged or ordered in some way to be intelligible. An unordered collection of observations or measurements permits no conclusions. If the data are few and simple, it is possible to derive tentative conclusions from a direct inspection, but the limitations for such inferences are quite severe. Only as the data are arranged in some kind of order and grouped in some kind of categories, do they become meaningful to us.

The method of classification used most frequently for quantitative data in psychology is a frequency distribution. This involves setting up categories for the data and tabulating the number of events falling within each category. In this manner a hundred test scores may be grouped into ten categories and a considerable economy of effort achieved, thereby, because most of us find it easier to remember the relative frequencies of ten categories than a hundred different scores. The rules for setting up such categories in psychological research are generous but the rules of logic demand that categories be meaningful, mutually exclusive, and exhaustive. The principle of classification should be explicit, permitting a single event to be assigned to one category and one category only, and the categories should permit tabulation of all such events possible. In brief, any categories established for the simplification of complex data should be consistent and uniform; they should not be based on whimsy.

DESCRIBING GROUPS

The characteristics of a group may be described either graphically or mathematically. Graphic methods, such as the bar graph and the pie graph, are commonly used to depict the features of some group. We are able to see quickly and easily the proportion of the group falling in certain categories, and we quickly gain an understanding of the relative significance or importance of certain features. Graphic methods are used widely because they permit an ease of communication and because they facilitate an understanding of group characteristics.

The well-known line graph or frequency polygon is a method of describing group characteristics by showing the distribution of the group on some continuous scale. The line which has been plotted with reference to two axes depicts the relationship between the frequency of occurrence and the degree or amount of the variable under consideration. The line, in effect, describes the group of observations or individuals with respect to a given characteristic. However, the ease with which the frequency distribution is understood often obscures the economy and convenience of describing the group more precisely with mathematical indices.

Although quite revealing in its description of the group, the line in a frequency polygon may be reduced to four relatively simple indices which convey the same information. Each of the indices represents one of the four characteristics of the line identified as (1) central tendency, (2) variation, (3) skewness or lack of symmetry, and (4) kurtosis or peakedness.

Central tendency may be defined as the clustering of events around some central point on a continuous scale. In measuring the height of a large group of men selected randomly from a busy street corner, we would quickly find that most of the men were between 5½ and 6 feet; some would be taller and some would be shorter, but most would cluster around some point on our yardstick, possibly the 5 ft., 8 in. mark. The arithmetic mean of the distribution of measurements could be computed to provide us with a simple index of this tendency. Now we could economize a bit in memory by retaining the information that the average height of the sample of men was 5 ft., 8 in.; it would not be necessary for us to remember the individual heights of all the men. Other indices of central tendency that we could compute would be the mode and the median; the mode is the height which occurs most frequently and the median is the point on our yardstick which divides the sample so that half of the sample falls above it and the other half falls below. In the normal probability curve that we have discussed previously, the mean, median, and mode all fall at the same point on our yardstick.

The arithmetic mean fails to represent the group as accurately as we usually desire, however, and we need an index of variation to show the tendency of the group to vary from the point of central tendency. In short, the group tends to cluster but it also tends to disperse or spread out. Several indices of variation have been worked out for our use; the simplest is the range of measurements which is computed by subtracting the lowest score in our distribution from the highest score and adding one. The most commonly used index, however, is called the standard deviation. We may not always remember that the standard deviation is the square root of the mean squared deviations from the mean but we should not have a great deal of trouble in recalling that the standard deviation is an index of variation from the point of central tendency. To make a long but interesting story short and bearable, the standard deviation is an indication of how much variation we have seen in our measurements; the larger the index the more the measurements vary, the smaller the index the more they cluster.

The indices of skewness and kurtosis need not detain us long. They are simple to compute and provide us with information about the leaning of the distribution toward one end of the continuum or the other and the tendency of the distribution to peak sharply or hang flatly over the horizontal axis.

In short, four easily computed indices will contain all the information given by the frequency polygon. Given these indices, we can reproduce the frequency distribution if the need arises, but more importantly we have substituted four numerical indices for the graph. Most of us give up our graphic methods of representation reluctantly but once indoctrinated to the precision and accuracy of descriptive mathematics, we appreciate their economy of thought and effort.

The crux of descriptive statistics then is that they give us a means of describing group characteristics with a precision and accuracy unobtainable by other methods. A teacher in describing her class may state simply that they are a nice group of children. If the situation is social and the talk small, her description would be adequate. If, however, the situation were "professional," her description would be highly inappropriate; we would need more precise information before we could conclude anything meaningful about the class. If she tells us that the mean intelligence quotient of the class is 125 with a standard deviation of 10, we believe she has told us something.

The advantages of precise description are quickly seen when it becomes necessary to compare the behavior or performance of two or more groups. The teacher with the "nice" children may have considerable difficulty determining if someone else's class is "nicer." Her description does not permit comparison of her class with another and any effort to do so would probably bog down in the kind of opinionated verbalizing that stultifies constructive thought.

The comparison of groups is basic to the testing of hypotheses in psychology. We have seen that the experimental approach hinges upon a comparison of performance by the same group under different conditions or the comparison of two or more groups assumed to be comparable in all relevant respects except the independent variable. While the collection of data may be experimental in either situation, the analysis of the data involves the use of statistical techniques. The dependent variable usually permits the computation of an arithmetic mean for each of the experimental groups and it is usually the mean performance of the groups that we compare to determine the effectiveness of the independent variable.

Statistical testing of hypotheses begins with the hypothesis that the observed difference between two groups is due to chance. This is known as the null hypothesis. Another way of stating it is to say that there are no differences between the two groups which cannot be accounted for by chance alone. By the rules of statistical logic, if we are able to reject the null hypothesis, then we may entertain the hypothesis that the difference between the two groups is due to the operation of the independent variable. This method of testing hypotheses has all the earmarks of "backing into a conclusion," but it returns to our earlier discussion of sampling error and probability. The probability that the difference observed between two groups is an effect of the independent variable is a function of the sampling error involved in selecting subjects for participation in the experiment. If sampling error is large the observed difference will be unstable and we cannot place trust in it; if sampling error is small, the probability that the observed difference is "an honest one" is high. When the latter is true, the observed difference between the two groups is said to be statistically significant.

The comparison of groups then is, in effect, a matter of testing statistically the observed differences between the groups. Numerous statistical tests have been devised for this purpose but the basic rationale for all of them is the same: Is the observed difference large enough so that we cannot attribute it to chance? If it is and if we have designed our experiment carefully and controlled the operation of extraneous variables, then we may attribute the difference in performance to the effect of the independent variable.

Comparative techniques in statistics permit more than a comparison of groups; they also enable us to compare the performance of an individual to the performance of a group. These methods are the basis for virtually all forms of psychological measurement. Psychological processes are not accessible to direct measurements as in physical dimensions such as length, weight, intensity, and duration, but when they can be scaled on a continuous dimension, we do have a means of comparing the individual with others if we can assign him a rank or a position on the scale. The measurements of the psychologist, therefore, are seldom direct but the advantages of being able to compare the performance of an individual with that of a known reference group are practically synonymous with those of measurement.

QUANTIFYING RELATIONSHIPS

One of the greatest advantages of statistical techniques to psychology lies in the methods that have been developed to specify the degree of relationship existing between continuous variables. Experimental methods usually enable the psychologist to determine if the independent and dependent variables are related, but unless the psychologist has varied both variables over a wide range, he is not able to specify the degree of relationship. Most experimental designs are geared to detect the presence or absence of a relationship, not to quantify it.

Correlational techniques have been devised to quantify the extent to which two variables vary concomitantly. They provide a simple index of relationship which tells us how much the two variables are related and in what way. The relationship may be positive in the sense that an increase in one variable is accompanied by an increase in the other or it may be negative in that an increase in one variable is accompanied by a decrease in the second. The direction of the relationship, however, is independent of the magnitude of the relationship. We may encounter large or small negative relationships as well as large or small positive ones. Frequently, the psychologist is not as interested in the direction of the relationship as its magnitude.

The advantages of being able to quantify the degree of the relationship may not be immediately apparent but possibly no other mathematical technique has been as useful to a science of behavior. If we consider the numerous characteristics in which people differ, we can appreciate the advantages of specifying how much any two of the characteristics covary. We are aware that height and weight are related to each other but there are enough short, fat people and tall, skinny people to make it convenient to quantify the relationship between height and weight. For large samples of men or women, the relationship is both positive and substantial but it is not perfect, and given the height of an individual, we do not automatically know his weight. We can estimate the weight of a person, however, if we know how much weight is related to height.

The estimation of one variable from another is equivalent to predicting the second variable from the first. In the case of independent and dependent variables, if we know the relationship between the two, we can predict the dependent variable from our observation and measurement of the independent variable. In situations where the independent variable precedes the dependent variable in time by an appreciable period, the advantages of predicting the outcome of the dependent variable is of great importance. Although the usefulness of correlational techniques in psychology is not limited to prediction purposes, this use of correlational methods is one of psychology's most significant achievements.

Statistics and Experimental Design

We have seen in our discussion of multivariate designs that the ties between statistics and experimentation are inseparable. Experimentation in psychology requires careful control and manipulation of experimental variables, but it also requires detailed statistical analysis of research data. Statistical techniques are necessary tools in virtually all psychological experiments.

Some psychological problems may be handled statistically, however, when experimentation is not possible. Psychology has established a definite preference for experimental methods when they are suitable, but the nature of psychology's subject matter sets limits on the problems which can be directly attacked with experimental methods. The individual differences of people are quite difficult to investigate experimentally but they have been studied with considerable profit by statistical methods. Intelligence testing, for example, grew from laboratory procedures for studying mental processes, but the development of the tests and other forms of psychological measurement has been within the framework of statistics rather than experimental psychology.

In one respect a statistical study may be considered an ex post facto experiment. This implies simply that the psychologist has not designed an experiment specifying in advance the observations he will make but rather he has analyzed data which was collected previously for other purposes. Whatever else our society does, it spends much time and effort keeping records. Birth records, school records, medical records, military records, and work records are just a few of the many mines of collected data that are reworked from time to time by statistical tools. From the standpoint of systematic inquiry, the data of such records always have a certain incompleteness.

But psychologists do not look the gift horse of public records in the mouth and they certainly do not complain if the teeth have no gold fillings. Much that has been recorded for other purposes can be studied with profit. Case records of students counseled in a university counseling bureau may be analyzed to determine the effect of counseling upon subsequent academic performance; tape recordings of counseling interviews may be used to test hypotheses about counseling processes and the effectiveness of counseling techniques; employment records may be studied to evaluate the validity of personnel selection devices.

The statistical approach may be contrasted with experimental methods in yet another way. If in the experimental setting the psychologist is primarily concerned with the establishment of functional relationships between experimental variables and behavioral variables, the statistical approach provides a means of studying in profitable detail the interrelationships of the behavioral variables. Or stated another way, if the experimental setting is designed to establish stimulus-response laws, the statistical approach provides response-response laws. Correlational techniques are unusually well suited for determining the relationships between the numerous behavioral variables we may observe and record. Even in the most carefully designed experiments subjects will often give more than one kind of response and the degree to which the different responses are related is a matter of no small consequence to psychology as a science.

The development of psychological tests has provided a multitude of responses suitable for correlational analysis. Traits and characteristics such as intelligence, abilities, aptitudes, interests, temperament, opinions, and attitudes are, in effect, behavioral variables; they are assessed either by the responses the subjects themselves make to the psychological tests and inventories or by the ratings or judgments made by observers. The interrelationships of such response variables have provided psychology with the kind of information which is essential to an understanding of individual differences and have, to no slight degree, formed the basis for differential psychology.

Factor analysis, a statistical method of analyzing intercorrelations, has greatly accelerated the analysis of behavioral variables in psychology. High-speed computers have made the correlation of numerous variables possible and factor analyses have provided a means of condensing enormous amounts of data back to manageable size. The objective of factor analytic techniques originally was to abstract underlying dimensions of a large number of correlations which would account for the variation observed in the numerous response variables, but more recently factorial methods have been used to identify underlying factors or dimensions of attitudes, interests, aptitudes, and abilities. The use of such techniques in the study of intelligence and personality characteristics has led to the development of theories of intelligence and personality based on factor analysis. In short, not only have factor analysis methods given psychology a means of describing economically the variables which are operative in complex behavior, but they have provided a means of exploring in considerable depth the underlying structure of intelligence and personality.

Fundamentals of
Psychological Measurement

We have seen previously that measurement in psychology is essentially a process of comparing the performance of an individual with that of a known reference group. The result is not so much a statement of how much of a given psychological characteristic the individual possesses as it is a way of ranking the individual in a group. The indirectness of psychological measurement has greatly disturbed the critics of psychology but we may attribute most of their disturbance to a misunderstanding of measurement in general.

Quantification of any characteristic may be said to begin with a notion of categories. Once we begin to think in terms of either A or non-A and once we place the categories in some kind of order, we have the rudiments of a measurement scale. Our scale becomes a bit more sophisticated when we begin to think in terms of degrees of the characteristic. The degree may be roughly described in qualitative terms such as "a great deal," but the detection of differences in degree or amount is a second step.

A third phase of measurement is entered when we are able to rank subjects or objects in some kind of order. Rocks may be ranked according to hardness, girls according to beauty, and politicians according to fidelity to campaign promises. Our ranks would be relative, of course, to the group of objects or subjects involved but we would not be dealing with properties of absolute amount. Hardness, beauty, and fidelity are always relative to some norm or reference that we have established.

The fourth phase of measurement which has been entered by a select few is one in which the amount of a characteristic is expressed in uniform units. This form of measurement is actually a process of automatic counting; it implies that we have a means of counting the number of units present. A ruler gives us a quick count of the number of inches involved in a given length.

Most psychological processes and characteristics are not amenable to the fourth phase of measurement because of the difficulty in establishing a zero point and uniform units. The difficulties of a zero point have been overcome in most forms of psychological measurement by substituting a known but arbitrary reference point, usually the arithmetic mean of some group. Units of relative uniformity are then established by adjusting the scores of individuals for the variation observed in a group of individuals. The result is an interesting creature of the psychometrician's ingenuity known as a standard score. The social standing of standard scores is not always high, even within the family of psychologists, but they have a usefulness which has not been surpassed by any other method. It helps to remember that a standard score is simply a means of adjusting the individual's performance by the mean performance and variation of some known reference group and there is little need to lose sleep over its status in the fourth phase of measurement. The point is that it is a convenient method of comparing individuals and groups; it is also a means of comparing different characteristics of the same individual. If it doesn't meet the physicist's standards of measurement, it will still serve many a purpose of the psychologist.

The Clinical
Approach in
Psychology   7

Clinical methods of inquiry differ from experimental and statistical methods by focusing directly on the individual. Both experimental and statistical investigations seek to establish relationships between variables, but they do not relate either the variables or the relations among them to a particular person. Neither the experimental psychologist nor the statistical psychologist tries to understand and explain the behavior of specific individuals; they seek the uniformities or regularities of behavior which will contribute to the understanding and explanation of behavior in general.

The clinical approach in psychology may be said to be the study of individuals. It is both an effort to integrate many kinds of information about a single person and an attempt to derive psychological facts which are relevant to the understanding of all persons. The focus is nonetheless on the individual person who is the object of study at a particular time. There is no attempt to relate variables by using a cross-section of people, but often the psychologist tries to explain a person by using a cross-section of variables. Although general principles concerning similar persons may be formulated in the process, the formulation of such principles may be secondary.

We have seen previously that science deals with abstractions, general principles, or universal laws; it seeks the uniformities of nature and not the events which are unique. Yet, in the individual person psychology is confronted with a unique event of such significance that despite its uniqueness, every effort must be made to deal with the event within the framework of natural science. Science has provided thousands of abstracted dimensions on which persons differ. These dimensions are biological, physiological, physical, and biochemical, as well as psychological; in fact, individual differences have been revealed in virtually every characteristic of human beings studied by science.

The study of a single person is not, of course, the exclusive domain of psychology. Both novelists and biographers have developed procedures for studying individuals from the standpoint of literature and history. Both devote their efforts to the particular person, showing him as the focal point of a larger social or cultural event. Both trace the individual's growth or development over a period of time but stress the underlying continuity of the person and the unity of his character or personality. Both try to give insight into the person's behavior by depicting specific, concrete events in the person's life. Both present what could be called a theory of the person.

Medical science skirts the study of individual persons when it points out the importance of a patient's social, economic, or cultural circumstances as well as his symptoms. The physician, as a scientist, seeks to identify and isolate the relevant symptoms of the patient and to arrive at an objective diagnosis, but medicine is frequently said to be an art as well as a science and this implies that the physician must treat the patient along with his symptoms.

The apparent dilemma between science's search for universal laws and psychology's concern with individual differences is an old one. Many have tried to resolve the issue by labeling science as nomothetic and fiction or biography as idiographic. This implies that psychology can be a science only as long as it seeks general principles or laws of behavior; once it stoops to consider the individuality of a subject, it has aligned itself with literature or biography, and it should not expect to be invited back to the house of science. The dilemma is fictitious.

Like all dilemmas, the issue between psychology as a science of behavior and psychology as a study of persons is posed as if we must choose one or the other. Fortunately, we may choose both for there is no reason why psychology cannot study both behavior and persons. Certainly, one of the better established generalizations in psychology pertains to the uniqueness of individuals, and there is no inconsistency in seeking other psychological principles or generalizations by studying unique persons. The two approaches are complementary rather than contradictory: the conclusions of experimental and statistical research are undoubtedly relevant to the study of persons and the study of persons, with or without plans to formulate universal laws, is pertinent to a science of behavior.

We are deceived into posing a dilemma only if we do not recognize that both universal and unique are relative concepts where human beings are concerned.

Methods of Clinical Inquiry

The use of the term clinical to designate the study of individual persons is not completely satisfactory. The origin of the usage is medical, and the term still suggests that observation and study of individuals are limited to the medical setting. Such a usage is hardly the one implied here, and it is seldom the usage intended by others when they speak of clinical psychology. Other terms have been suggested as replacements but not accepted; we still refer to the study of a single person as a clinical study.

NATURAL OBSERVATION

We have seen that the study of persons begins with natural observation. All of us are in position to observe the behavior of others in many situations and we seldom fail to form theories or hypotheses about the acts of particular persons. Our efforts as amateur psychologists are frequently unsophisticated but are nonetheless the rudiments of clinical inquiry.

Natural observation as a method of clinical inquiry may be illustrated by the reaction we have when seeing a person for the first time. Despite the fact that we may see him only once and then only for a very brief time, we may be left with impressions which are "lasting" and we may spin many a fanciful notion of the kind of person he is. Even in the briefest contact we may respond to a dozen different facets of his individuality.

We may notice his physical appearance either as a total pattern or in considerable detail. In the first instance we recall later that he was "nice looking" but cannot specify in what particular way; in the second, we may become quite analytic and deduce from his physical features something of his life story. Sherlock Holmes, in meeting Dr. Watson for the first time, deduced immediately that Watson had just returned from Afghanistan. Holmes explained his inference as a series of deductions springing from his observations of Dr. Watson, but speaks of them running so swiftly through his mind that he was hardly conscious of the steps involved. Our inferences of others are seldom as dramatic or direct as those of Holmes, but his is the example par excellence of astute powers of observation and inference.

CLINICAL OBSERVATION

The study of the mentally retarded, emotionally disturbed, criminally insane, and other persons with acute behavioral disorders is a necessary adjunct to the study of normal persons. Like all other growth or developmental processes, behavior may become pathological, and the implications of abnormal behavior for an understanding of normal behavior must be considered by a science of behavior. It is no longer thought that the study of the mentally retarded and the emotionally disturbed is ideal because the mental processes are slowed down in one and the emotional reactions are speeded up in the other, but the underlying continuity of most behavioral disorders with normal behavior stresses their mutual relevance.

The clinical observation of behavioral disorders is complex and often uncontrolled, but the purposes of clinical observation are essentially the same as those of experimental observation; the psychologist seeks to identify, isolate, and relate the relevant variables in the subject's behavior. The variables operative in the clinical setting, however, are often subtle and may be regarded as no more than cues while the functional relationships sought between the relevant variables may be no more than hunches or guesses. Much of the difficulty stems from the fact that frequently the psychologist's objectives in the clinical setting are dual; the psychologist is often trying to observe and study the subject's behavior at the same time that he is trying to change or modify the behavior. The extent to which active participation with the subject disrupts the psychologist's objectivity as an observer is debatable, but there is no reason why the psychologist cannot apply the best of scientific principles in studying clinical behavior while other psychologists work with their clinical subjects.

CLINICAL INTERVIEWING

Self-report by the subject is admissible evidence in the clinical approach. This demonstrates, no doubt, the inability of psychology to escape reliance on introspection as a source of information. But actually, introspection in a clinical interview is not identical with the form of introspection developed by the structuralists. In clinical study the psychologist is seldom interested in the content of a subject's consciousness as influenced by variation in physical stimuli but rather the feelings and attitudes which apparently underly the subject's "perception of reality." The subject may be asked to describe his feelings and attitudes, but more often he is asked to discuss his responses and experiences of the past. The subject's recall of past experiences provides data which are unavailable by any other method. Others may describe the events in which the subject was involved, but only the subject can give us any indication as to what he remembers or doesn't remember about past events. More importantly, the subject's discussion of past events may reflect attitudes and feelings which are still present. When discussing his relations with parents, teachers, or bosses, the facts recalled by the subject may or may not be "true." However, the manner in which he recalls his transactions with them may reveal much that is significant about his attitudes and feelings toward those who exercise some degree of control over his life.

Self-report by the subject is not a substitute for direct observation but rather another source of information. The psychologist must assume in many situations that the subject is both able and willing to give the desired information, but even more important he must be alert to reflected attitudes and feelings. Information about these aspects of the subject's behavior is difficult to gain in any other way, and it is often present even when the subject himself is being "objective." In fact, we might say that the subject tells us something every time he opens his mouth; the question is "what?"

PSYCHOLOGICAL TESTING

Standardized tests, questionnaires, and inventories are an abundant source of information about the psychological characteristics of individuals. As noted previously, psychological measurements provide a means of comparing the individual with others, and from the comparisons the psychologist is often able to derive some of the most pertinent information about his subject. Information about the subject's intelligence, personality traits, educational achievement, vocational aptitudes, skills and abilities, occupational interests, personal preferences, opinions, attitudes, and beliefs is frequently gained by use of psychometric tests.

Standardized tests differ from other methods of clinical assessment in that they have been standardized on other individuals; they are objective in the sense that they can be scored by clerical personnel and statistically analyzed. They are said to be trait-and-factor centered because they are assumed to measure underlying structures of the individual's behavior and because they are usually interpreted in terms of scores rather than in terms of the psychological processes involved.

Psychological testing is closer to experimental methods of inquiry than other clinical methods because it permits planned, controlled observation of the subject's behavior in much the same manner that experimentation does. There are, needless to say, limitations to testing but the method has the advantage of sampling the subject's behavior systematically; it is an effort to elicit specific responses from the subject. Spontaneous and random behavior on the part of the subject may be of great interest to the psychologist, but psychological testing provides an opportunity for observation which he can control.

SPECIALIZED TRICKS OF THE TRADE

Psychologists have been quite prolific in the production of supplementary methods and techniques for clinical assessment. These include semistandardized tests, sentence-completion blanks, personal-data forms, case-history forms, projective techniques, and a variety of methods for analyzing behavioral products such as drawings, diaries, poetry, and autobiographies. The validity and reliability of such methods vary greatly from technique to technique and their use is mostly a matter of preference with the individual psychologist. The fact that some psychologists use some techniques extensively while other psychologists do not suggests that interaction effects between psychologist and technique may be quite large. Some psychologists apparently elicit the information they desire by using certain techniques while other equally well-trained psychologists draw blanks.

The use of projective techniques for clinical assessment is one of the most interesting episodes in the history of psychology. The rationale may be described as a variation on the old theme of introspection. The procedure consists of presenting the subject with an ambiguous stimulus complex, the assumption being that the subject will "make sense" out of the ambiguity by projecting into the stimulus complex his own feelings, wishes, thoughts, desires, motives, and internal conflicts. The assumption is similar to the one in clinical interviewing where we believe that we can tell something about the subject's feelings and attitudes from the way he talks about events in his past. The assumption cuts much deeper in projective techniques, however, and relates to the Freudian concept of repression. The information given in a clinical interview is replete with omissions and distortions because there is much that the subject cannot or will not reveal about himself if he can help it. By presenting him with a stimulus which is unstructured, the psychologist assumes that the subject will unwittingly reveal his repressed motives, interests, and fears. The assumption is well taken, but the validity of the psychologist's inferences from the subject's "projections" is a matter of considerable issue in contemporary psychology. Future developments will no doubt illuminate the issue better than past developments have, but in the meantime psychologists are divided into three camps about projective techniques—those who believe in them, those who do not, and those who don't care one way or the other.

Methods of
Clinical Inference

It is no doubt evident from the preceding discussion that in clinical methods of inquiry the psychologist himself is often the recording instrument. Physical scientists have learned to be distrustful of their observational abilities, and they have sought diligently to relieve themselves of as many of their observing, reading, and recording duties as possible. Astronomers no longer look at the stars; they study photographs. And yet, psychology in its present stage of development is forced to rely heavily upon the perception and judgment of the psychologist when we study individuals. The psychologist's own reactions are a part of his data, and even though he uses the best of interview techniques, the most carefully standardized tests, and the most careful analysis of behavioral products, the psychologist must sooner or later synthesize his information into meaningful conclusions about the individual. His skill in doing so is the essence of clinical inquiry.

The problem of synthesis after analysis has plagued psychology from the beginning. The associationists, the structuralists, and the functionalists were able to break mind down but couldn't put it back together. Factor analysis has continued to yield underlying factors or behavioral dimensions, and psychologists of psycho-analytic bent have continued to postulate needs, urges, and impulses, but neither has shown signs of returning from their diverging tours. Only the Gestalt psychologists have avoided the problem by declining to take an analytic approach.

Small wonder, then, that in recent years there has been an increasing suspicion that an extremely analytic orientation may disrupt the perception and judgment of others. Excessive reliance on specific methods of clinical inquiry and tenacity to a particular theoretical orientation may limit the psychologist's understanding of the person and may dull the usefulness of his conclusions. The identification of relevant variables may become a result of the psychologist's mental set rather than a means of explaining the individual's behavior. Psychologists have been known to observe "what the theory demands" and not what actually occurred. Does this signify a return to intuitive, impressionistic methods in studying individuals? No, the struggle to develop valid and reliable methods of clinical inquiry has been a difficult but profitable one, and it is not likely that it will be put aside. It does pose the problem, however, of developing the psychologist's sensitivities to the subject's behavior while correcting or modifying them with more objective methods. The psychologist may gain information by the short cuts of intuition but we can never trust his conclusions until we can arrive there by retracing his steps with better established rules of inference.

CLINICAL HYPOTHESES

If inference is an inevitable component of observations of others, it would appear that the psychologist's observations of individual subjects is an exceedingly valuable source of hypotheses concerning human behavior. Clinical hypotheses may be formulated on the basis of sociocultural, historical, or comparative information about the individual.

In the case of hypotheses derived from sociocultural knowledge, the psychologist may be said to attribute to the individual specific characteristics generally associated with the groups or organizations to which he belongs. This form of hypothesis, which is dependent upon the psychologist's familiarity with the empirical findings and insights of sociology and cultural anthropology, assumes that cultural determinants are of major importance in understanding the individual. It implies that the individual's behavior can be understood by identifying the social, ethnic, economic, political, educational, occupational, religious, national, and regional factors in his life; the various groups of which he is a member and his various roles in those groups are of major concern. In brief, having learned that a person is white, of Anglo-Saxon descent, a member of the Republican Party, a graduate of Harvard University, a former resident of Connecticut, and a management trainee at General Motors, we may form some rather accurate hypotheses concerning the person as an individual.

In much the same manner, by tracing the individual's growth and development, the psychologist is often able to form hypotheses concerning the sequential effects of the subject's previous experiences. Having learned that the subject's early experiences in a certain type of home environment were followed by several years of scholastic difficulties and eventual departure from school before completion of the eighth grade, and that these experiences, in turn, were followed by a series of menial jobs from which the subject was often discharged for tardiness or absenteeism, the psychologist may be able to formulate hypotheses concerning the subject's "career pattern" or "life style." From his formulations he may infer "the next step" that the subject will most likely take.

If the primary method of clinical inference in a sociocultural approach is deductive and that of the historical or developmental approach inductive, then the comparative study of the individual may be regarded as a combination of deductive and inductive inference. The most obvious form of comparative study is conducted by means of psychological tests. As we have seen, the gist of psychological measurement is the comparison of the individual with persons in a known reference group. Here the psychologist is concerned with the individual's relative standing in the group and assesses the person in terms of that individual's deviation from the norms established by groups. By comparing the personality traits, intellectual capacities, aptitudes, interests, abilities, skills, motives, objectives, expectations, and other characteristics of the individual with those of other people, the psychologist is able to reach an understanding of the subject as a person as well as to formulate hypotheses concerning the interrelationships and implications of the subject's many dimensions.

It is obvious then that clinical methods of inquiry provide us with an abundance of hypotheses concerning human behavior. The observation of numerous individuals in a particular kind of setting and the observation of the same individual over a period of time inevitably results in hypotheses that are highly relevant for a science of behavior. The origins of the hypotheses are not always clear but a careful distinction between the origin of the hypothesis and the means of testing it would seem to be quite meaningful. The fact that a hypothesis does not readily submit to test makes it no less interesting as a hypothesis. It is only when we confuse clinical hypotheses with established fact that we do ourselves an injustice.

NOTIONS OF CAUSATION

No one is likely to argue that mere description of a person's behavior is sufficient for understanding and explanation. We are compelled to "go beyond our data" and seek some kind of explanatory concept or principle which will account for the behavior we observe. Even when our conclusions about a person may not be generalized to others, we often seek to extend the conclusions to other situations involving the same person. The necessity of generalizations in psychology is undeniable; like abstractions, they are with us always.

The plausibility of an explanation of an individual's behavior is a generalized description of the conditions necessary to produce and sustain his behavior. In one respect this means that we never really answer the question of why an individual behaves as he does but rather we provide an account of how he behaves. The conditions deemed necessary for even the simplest behavioral act are multiple and efforts to designate any of them as sufficient are rarely successful. The best notion of causation, therefore, seems to be one of specifying the conditions which must be antecedent to the individual's behavior. For this purpose we apparently need at least four classes of causal variables: (1) those pertaining to the individual's external environment, (2) those pertaining to his internal environment, (3) those pertaining to dispositional concepts, and (4) those describing capacities and abilities.

The variables in the subject's external environment include not only those of his physical surroundings but his social, religious, political, economic, and cultural environment as well. Included would be the situational, task, and treatment variables identified in the experimental setting. By the subject's internal environment we mean the variables in his physical, physiological, neurological, and biochemical make-up—in short, the variables of physical and biological sciences which are internal to the human organism.

The use of dispositional concepts in psychology is the most difficult of the four classes of causal variables to assess. These concepts refer to relatively enduring tendencies, proclivities, or inclinations of the human organism and include such psychological characteristics as interests, needs, attitudes, motives, drives, and personality traits. Because contemporary psychology has viewed man's behavior as primarily adaptive, these concepts have gained the attention of most psychologists dealing with individual persons and may be unduly emphasized in contemporary psychology.

Psychologists have had better success in dealing with variables describing capacities and abilities. Acquired knowledge or information and traits or factors such as intelligence, sensory acuities, motor skills, perceptual capacities, and vocational aptitudes have proved more amenable to psychological measurement, but they have not caught the imagination and interest of many psychologists. They are sometimes referred to as static concepts and thereby contrasted with the more dynamic concepts of motivation and needs. Indeed, there is a gratuitous assumption that behavior is adequately explained when a need or motive is identified, and the efforts of some psychologists to catalogue needs is strangely reminiscent of earlier efforts to classify instincts. The disadvantage of both need and instinct as explanatory concepts is their circularity. The behavior by which the need is expressed is often the only means we have of detecting the need.

CLINICAL VERSUS STATISTICAL PREDICTION

An issue of considerable importance to contemporary psychology is the relative effectiveness of clinical prediction compared to that of statistical prediction. In his clinical study of the individual the psychologist is frequently asked to predict the individual's future behavior. Will the individual complete training satisfactorily? Will he adjust successfully to community life after serving time in the penitentiary? Will he benefit from psychotherapy? Will he be able to live a useful and productive life after release from a rehabilitation center? Should an excluded student be readmitted to college? Will a juvenile delinquent straighten up before it's too late?

The problems, needless to say, are those involving the complexities of human behavior. The question, however, is whether the psychologist, after making a clinical study, can make a better prognosis of the individual's later behavior than the psychologist's colleague who has not studied the individual but who has studied the frequency of certain behavior in given groups. For example, the statistically oriented psychologist may tabulate the frequency with which first offenders in a juvenile court reappear and in a particular case simply "play the percentages" of past observations. If six out of seven first offenders have further difficulties with the law, then he calculates that the odds are six to one that the juvenile now in question will reappear. Clinically, however, the psychologist may have made an intensive study of the individual and he may try to predict no further difficulties with the "law" on the basis of his understanding of the particular person. The question is which method gives the better results?

The answer is not an easy one and the issue of clinical versus statistical prediction will undoubtedly remain with psychology for years to come. Such evidence as is now available has been embarrassing to psychologists seeking to predict from an understanding of the individual. This is disturbing, to say the least, but it cannot be accepted as a final answer. The complexity of the variables in prediction has often been underestimated, but the issue involved may well strike at the very heart of the clinical approach in psychology.

The Dual Role
of Psychology   8

The rapid development of psychology in the twentieth century has not been without growing pains. If psychology began as an activity cloistered behind ivy covered walls, it soon found that it could not remain there. Two world wars have forced psychology to play an increasing role in the world of public affairs, and psychology has become a profession as well as a science.

The First World War brought psychologists out of their secluded laboratories to help mobilize the nation's manpower. For the first time in the nation's history it was necessary to select, classify, and place thousands of men in military service. The tools and techniques developed by psychologists for the measurement of individual differences proved to be highly adaptable to the problems of mobilization, and psychologists found themselves submerged in the mental testing movement. They did not always steer the movement but they did provide the technical know-how.

The momentum gathered in World War I was transferred in postwar years to the nation's educational, industrial, and social institutions. Colleges administered tests to applicants and beginning students; industry and business tested job applicants for selection and placement purposes; and public institutions gave tests in an effort to diagnose, classify, and treat inmates and patients more effectively. The depression of the thirties focused the nation's attention on the necessity of suitable job placement for the nation's workforce. Tests were developed to measure aptitudes and abilities, interests and vocational preferences, temperament and personality characteristics. The unemployed were tested, interviewed, and advised; the young were tested, counseled, and guided. The nation had become aware of the importance of work, and psychologists were the ones who could match men and jobs.

The Second World War accelerated psychology's concern with practical affairs. Once again it was necessary to mobilize the nation's manpower but on a much greater scale than before. The lessons learned in World War I and in the postwar and the depression years were applied to the problems of selection, classification, and placement, but the problems were intensified by the increasing complexity of war. For example, aviation had played a relatively small part in World War I, but it became a major element in the striking force in World War II. The highly skilled and technical duties of piloting, navigating, and bombardiering were a far cry from those of simple soldiering, and thus selection and classification were more important. Equally complicating was the fact that methods of selection soon reached their natural limitations. As airplanes which flew faster and faster were developed, it was no longer adequate to select young men of high sensory acuity and quick motor reaction; there were not enough of the young men to go around, and even their reaction time was slow with planes rapidly approaching supersonic speeds. The challenge had to be met with better equipment design and better training methods. The machinery and equipment of war had to be adapted to man's sensory capacities and motor skills; better methods of training perceptual discrimination and motor response had to be devised. Selection, classification, and placement were still essential, but training and human engineering were equally urgent.

Long before World War II was over, it had become evident that the services of psychologists were needed not only to mobilize manpower but also to return the men to civilian life. The identification of men mentally or emotionally unsuited for the pressures and tensions of war became the major concern of many psychologists in military service; the reeducation of those with physical disabilities and the retraining and treatment of those with behavioral disorders became of greater importance as the war continued. With the war's end and the return of millions of servicemen to civilian life, the problems of readjusting to the community, locating suitable employment, deriving benefit from educational and training opportunities, and rehabilitating those physically or emotionally handicapped by the war became acute.

It is understandable, therefore, that with the close of World War II psychology found itself cast in the dual role of science and profession. The die was cast and much as psychology might have preferred better preparation for its role as a profession, the demand for psychological services could not be denied. Psychologists had shown a capacity for adaptability and resourcefulness; now they were asked not only to further man's knowledge of his own behavior but to apply that knowledge to the problems of education, government, industry, commerce, and mental health.

The Division of
Psychological Labor

There is no method of classification which will do justice to the diversity of contemporary psychology as a scientific endeavor. Psychologists are currently at work on such a diversity of problems that any categories set up on the basis of problems could not hope to be well defined, mutually exclusive, and exhaustive. Nor does it help to classify psychology by areas of endeavor; psychologists interested in the problems of education often refer to themselves as educational psychologists, but few psychologists at work in the field of learning theory refer to themselves as educational psychologists. Most classification schemes devised for psychology make no attempt to be consistent; they cut across problems, areas, methods, and place of employment. Yet, there seems to be a fairly clear-cut manner in which psychologists have divided their labor and to which they owe an intellectual allegiance. The individual psychologist may not agree with the way he has been classified, but a close examination of his work, the kinds of problems he deals with, the procedures he follows in studying the problems, and the principles or conclusions he derives from his study will usually suggest how he may be classified. The dimension of classification, for want of a more catchy title, may be referred to as "predominant orientation to method."

By method we may specify one of the three approaches we have discussed in the past three chapters—experimental, statistical, and clinical. We have stressed, however, that the three methods are rapidly reaching rapprochement and the combination of experimental-statistical, statistical-clinical, and experimental-clinical methods is becoming commonplace. It is not suggested, therefore, that the use of any method is exclusive or that psychology may be classified by method employed; the principle of classification is the psychologist's orientation to method and because he may use a combination of methods, we add the modifying adjective "predominant."

In brief, then, the efforts of contemporary psychology to further our knowledge of man's behavior may be classified as to the method which consistently plays the major role in the acquisition of that knowledge. Despite the fact that psychologists may cut across areas of inquiry, dealing with different kinds of problems and employing different procedures, they may be observed to maintain an orientation to either experimental, statistical, or clinical methods. This orientation is apparently maintained because certain problems have been handled traditionally within the framework of one or the other method, and because that method apparently carries final authority for resolution of the problem. The grist for the psychological mill is still experimental, statistical, or clinical data.

EXPERIMENTAL PSYCHOLOGY

The problems of major concern in experimental psychology are those of sensation, perception, learning, motivation, and thinking. Historically, experimental psychology has been influenced greatly by the schools of functionalism, behaviorism, and Gestalt psychology. Psychophysical methods are still used extensively in experimental psychology, and considerable effort has been made in recent years to test psychoanalytic hypotheses by laboratory methods. Within the framework of experimental psychology, extensive theories of learning and motivation have been developed by a group of psychologists known as neobehaviorists; theories of perception have been developed by a group known as cognitive theorists. Lesser attention has been devoted to thinking, possibly because it was tainted with mentalism, but interest in the topic has been greatly revived in recent years. Research with electronic digital computers has stimulated investigations of memory-coding, problem-solving, and decision-making processes that would have been taboo in the wake of Watsonian behaviorism. The Gestalt psychologists contributed exploratory or descriptive studies of thinking but only recently has there been any genuine promise of an analytic, systematic attack on thinking as a psychological process.

Even more promising, perhaps, are the broadening concepts of motivation. No longer restricted to concepts of motivation derived from physiological states or tissue needs, many experimental psychologists appear both able and willing to treat motivation as the direction of behavior toward dealing with the environment; the urge to perceive, explore, manipulate, and achieve is as relevant as the need to maintain physiological stability.

Several subspecialties may be identified within the framework of experimental psychology, the most notable of which are comparative, physiological, and engineering psychology. Comparative psychology is concerned with similarities and differences of behavior among biological species. Because of the more rigorous control of situational and subject variables permissible in research with animals, comparative psychology has contributed greatly to the mainstream of psychology. Comparative and physiological techniques are often combined in investigations of learning, perception, and motivation, but for the most part comparative psychologists are identified by their choice of animals as subjects, and physiological psychologists are known for their choice of neurophysiological concepts as experimental variables. Both employ rigorous experimental controls and insist on a high degree of objectivity in description and explanation.

Engineering psychology is the outgrowth of concern with the adaptation of situational variables to man's capacities and abilities. If the early functionalists saw the organism striving to adapt to environmental demands, engineering psychologists have seen the necessity of adapting man's environment to human demands. Although dealing with a broad range of problems, engineering psychology is best illustrated by its efforts to design machines, equipment, and other instruments which are compatible with man's sensory, perceptual, and motor capacities. Space travel is contingent upon man's ability to carry an appropriate bit of environment with him; how well man succeeds in adapting that bit of environment to his many limitations will determine the conquest of space.

STATISTICAL PSYCHOLOGY

In statistical psychology we find that the problems of major concern cut across most areas of human endeavor. This is due, perhaps, to the fact that statistical methods have been adaptable to problems which do not permit an experimental or clinical investigation. The unifying concept, however, appears to be the study of individual differences and the relevant variables are such concepts as intelligence, abilities, aptitudes, interests, attitudes, opinions, beliefs, temperament, and personality.

If Germany is the ancestral home of experimental psychology, then England is the motherland of statistical psychology. Sir Francis Galton launched the study of individual differences and British statisticians have provided the majority of tools and techniques. Both German experimental psychology and British statistical psychology employed similar statistical concepts, but the two fields maintained a historical distinction well into the twentieth century.

Statistical psychology has contributed theories of intelligence and personality and, with the development of factor analysis, it has contributed an exceptionally potent research tool for dealing with such complex behavior as leadership, creativity, problem solving, and performance on perceptual-motor tasks. Even more important, perhaps, statistical psychology has contributed techniques for selection, classification, placement, evaluation, and assessment of people.

The great variety of subspecialties in statistical psychology has obscured the fact that statistical concepts are the foundation of the subspecialties. The more commonly known subspecialties may be designated as differential, vocational, educational, and industrial psychology. The first of these, differential psychology, is the study of differences in human traits and capacities among social groups, races, national origin groups, socioeconomic groups, age groups, and the two sexes. Differential psychology begins with the study of variation of human abilities but branches off into comparative studies of various groups. In many respects it is the underlying basis for vocational, educational, and industrial psychology.

Vocational psychology is a field relating the psychologist's knowledge of human capacities and characteristics to the demands and duties of various occupations. Industrial psychology may be said to be concerned with the larger implications of man's work environment. Not only does industrial psychology study the influence of environmental variables upon job proficiency and employee morale, but it investigates the far more complex variables of industrial organization, executive leadership, and industrial forces in general.

Educational psychology is the application of psychological principles and methods to the many problems of learning under formal instruction. The measurement of individual differences in learning capacities, the assessment of learning readiness and motivation, and the evaluation of academic progress are but a few of the educational problems to which psychological concepts and techniques are applied. More recently, through the introduction of pro-grammed instruction or "teaching machines," the contributions of psychology have been accelerated. Some psychologists believe that a technology of learning psychology has virtually revolutionized our traditional conceptions of education.

CLINICAL PSYCHOLOGY

The traditional concern of clinical psychology may be identified as the origin, growth, and development of behavior with particular regard for its irregularities or its deviations. The outlook of clinical psychology is longitudinal as opposed to the cross-sectional view-point of experimental and statistical psychology. The historical antecedents and parallels of clinical psychology are developmental or child psychology, psychopathology, and social psychology. Developmental psychology, as the name implies, is concerned with the development of behavior throughout the life span. Beginning with the study of prenatal behavior and development, it follows the course of behavior as it unfolds, develops, and matures. Behavior is viewed as a continuously changing process. The continuity of the process is studied as a series of stages, but attention is focused on the developmental changes which occur and the limitations placed on those changes by hereditary and environmental influences. Sometimes identified as genetic psychology, it has included in recent years the study of the decline of behavior in old age.

Abnormal psychology or psychopathology may be said to investigate the relevant variables of sensory defects, physical handicaps, emotional disturbance, mental retardation, and other psychological disabilities. This area of psychology has been greatly influenced by the school of psychoanalysis but its ancestral home is closer to France than Vienna.

The theoretical contributions of clinical psychology have been predominantly concerned with theories of personality. A unifying framework which would incorporate the psychologist's knowledge of heredity, neurophysiology, cultural factors, behavioral development, and psychological disabilities would be of valuable assistance in his efforts to understand the individual. Not only should such a theoretical framework provide explanatory concepts and principles but it should suggest methods of correcting or preventing behavioral disorders.

A Profession
of Psychology

If the lines between divisions of scientific psychology are sometimes blurred, the same is also true of the distinction between its role as a science and its role as a profession. Yet, the distinction between the two roles is an important one and the two contrasting roles should be delineated as carefully as possible. In discussing psychology's division of scientific labor, we have focused on its efforts to further our knowledge of human behavior; in discussing its activities as a profession, we must focus on its efforts to apply psychological principles and procedures to the problems of industry, business, government, education, and mental health. The difficulties of defining a profession are similar to those of defining science but we can avoid most of them simply by pointing out the distinctive features of a profession of psychology.

Psychology has specialized skills and knowledge. The primary requisite of a profession is the possession of specialized skills and knowledge which are not common to other professional fields; this implies that the profession must be able to make a unique contribution to society. The specialized skills and knowledge of psychology are its concepts and methods for the analysis and interpretation of behavior. Psychologists have developed instruments for measuring and recording behavior, techniques for diagnosing, assessing, and evaluating human performance in numerous areas of endeavor, and principles of behavior modification which have commendable appropriateness for the various problems for industry, business, education, and government.

Psychology has defined functions and responsibilities. This characteristic is related to the first one. Not only must the profession possess the ability to render public service but the service must be defined by society and the profession must be accorded responsibility for rendering the service. Usually this is accomplished through the passage of legislation which accords to a specific profession responsibility for defined functions. Long before legislation can be passed, however, society must "perceive" the advisability of placing responsibility in the hands of persons meeting certain qualifications. Briefly, the public must recognize the desirability of the service which can be offered and then it must take steps to protect its welfare in the matter. Licensing or certification is for the public's protection—not for the profession's benefit alone.

Where psychology has ventured professional services, it has had many imitators and considerable competition. In all probability there are more self-styled experts on human behavior than any other subject known to man. Several states have taken steps to protect the public from incompetent psychological services but anything approaching uniform public recognition throughout the nation is sadly missing. There is, however, a rapidly growing awareness of the services which can be rendered by professional psychologists and we may confidently predict that the future will bring better public recognition.

Psychology has national organization. In an era of mass communication the necessity for a national spokesman is fairly obvious. The role of a national organization, however, must be that of mediator between the profession and the public; if the national organization does not represent the public's interest as well as the profession, it quickly deteriorates into a mere pressure group and should be accorded no more respect than any other pressure group. The American Psychological Association fulfills the role of mediator for psychologists and the public. Organized in 1892, the APA now has over 20,000 members.

Psychology has standards of training and work experience. This function of a profession is sometimes referred to as the practice of professional birth control. It implies that a profession is able to regulate the training and educational programs which prepare persons to enter the profession. It further implies that a person will not be permitted to enter the professional field until he has graduated from an accredited educational program and fulfilled the specified requirements of supervised work experience and personal qualifications. The APA has established an Education and Training Board which sets standards of accreditation for graduate programs in psychology. The APA also has a Board of Professional Examiners who certify psychologists in the professional fields of clinical, counseling, and industrial psychology.

Psychology regulates the behavior of its members. This requisite of a profession implies that the members of the profession are obligated to meet certain standards of conduct. More often than not, the profession has articulated a code of ethics to which the members subscribe. Members who do not meet the expectations of the code in their professional conduct are subject to discipline by the profession. Depending on the strength of the profession's national organization, this could mean dismissal from the organization and possible revocation of licensure. The APA has adopted such a code of ethics and has sought diligently to help members of the psychological profession meet its expectations. In recent years the APA has dismissed members of the organization who were judged not to be acting in the public's best interest.

Areas of Psychological Service

Judged by its specialized skills and knowledge, its defined functions and responsibilities, its national representation, its standards of training and experience, and its regulation of member behavior, psychology would seem to have made exceptional progress in its rise to professional standing. Only in the matter of public recognition has there been a genuine lag.

Public recognition of the profession of psychology has been slow because of a certain amount of stimulus confusion. In looking at the psychologist, the layman has difficulty in discriminating the psychologist's functions from those of the psychiatrist, the psychoanalyst, and the psychiatric social worker. Although few in number, the psychoanalysts have had the better publicity. As mentioned earlier, psychoanalytic theory has influenced art, drama, and literature greatly, and as a result the general public has been exposed to psychoanalysts in novels, plays, and motion pictures. The stereotype of the bald, goateed, rotund psychoanalyst, wearing a cutaway coat and speaking with a Viennese accent, is now stock-in-trade for actors and cartoonists.

The psychiatrist and the psychologist are less easily stereotyped for the general public. The psychiatrist has the staff and serpent symbol, which belongs to all medical doctors, but his specialization in mental and emotional disorders has carried him some distance from general practice and he is likely to be identified by the general public as a "head shrinker" rather than a medical specialist. Both the psychiatrist and the psychologist need better recognition and understanding of their functions and responsibilities.

The professional psychologist has neither a couch nor a doctor of medicine degree. He should have, however, a doctor of philosophy degree from a reputable university with an accredited program in the field of his specialization. At the present there are three such fields in professional psychology and the psychologist may now be certified by the American Board of Examiners as a clinical, counseling, or industrial psychologist.

The clinical psychologist is concerned with the diagnosis, assessment, and treatment of behavioral disorders. His functions vary widely, however, and he may be employed by a variety of institutions, such as treatment and diagnostic centers, hospitals, mental institutions, penal institutions, community agencies, public schools, and private industry. In many cases the clinical psychologist may be engaged in private practice, working with individuals on a fee basis or accepting referrals from community organizations and institutions. Clinical psychologists are also employed extensively by governmental agencies, such as the military services, the Veterans Administration, and the Department of Health, Education, and Welfare.

Industrial psychologists are engaged in the application of psychological principles and methods to the various personnel problems of industrial, commercial, and financial organizations. They may be employed by a particular company or industry or they may be engaged in private consulting work, dealing with a variety of problems and working with many different business concerns. Traditionally the industrial psychologist deals with problems of personnel selection, placement, training, classification, promotion, and transfer. In recent years, however, he has become concerned with the larger aspects of work efficiency and job satisfaction, working with the problems of industrial organization, labor relations, and executive development. The industrial psychologist may also be employed by governmental agencies or engaged in such diverse activities as marketing research or public opinion polling.

In some respects the advent of the clinical and industrial psychologists may be regarded as the logical extension of clinical and statistical methods of inquiry to the world of practical affairs. Both may apply the general principles and findings of psychology to practical problems but the unique contribution of each would seem to be method rather than knowledge per se.

The middle ground between the clinical and industrial psychologists may be said to be occupied by the third professional group, the counseling psychologists. Although often confused with industrial and clinical psychology, the specialty of counseling psychology may be easily distinguished. Where clinical psychology is primarily concerned with the malfunctioning behavior of persons, the counseling psychologist works with the normal, diverse problems of adjustment and choice. The orientation of the clinical psychologist is therapeutic, whereas the orientation of the counseling psychologist is educational. In working with others, the counseling psychologist seeks to help the individual set goals of educational and vocational significance rather than those pertaining to personality organization. As a result the counseling psychologist is more likely to be employed in an educational institution, usually a counseling center for students. By virtue of his versatility, however, he may be employed in any of the institutions or organizations that use the services of a clinical or industrial psychologist. In some instances the counseling psychologist may be clinically oriented while in others he performs in harmony with the industrial psychologist. If his status at the present time is not as well defined as that of the clinical or industrial psychologist, it is due, undoubtedly, to the fact that the counseling psychologist has chosen to occupy the middle ground.

Prognosis and Prophecy

What can be said of psychology's future? Or better still, what can be said of its ability to continue to play a dual role as science and profession? An opinion survey of the nation's psychologists would undoubtedly show that psychologists are divided in their opinions of psychology's dual role. With science enjoying such prestige in American society, we could predict that most psychologists would identify themselves as scientists. But an even greater number would identify themselves as both scientists and professional persons. If we may judge from psychology's brief but versatile history, we certainly can predict that psychology will continue to display ingenuity and resourcefulness in its progress both as a science and a profession.

In the science of psychology there is considerable basis for optimism. Psychological research is expanding at a rate which could not have been visualized at the close of World War II. The combination of experimental methods with improved techniques of statistical analysis has proved unusually adaptable to research in virtually all areas of human behavior and conduct. These techniques permit the study of numerous, complex variables in situations more closely approximating "the realities of human society," and psychologists have become far less timid in their willingness to attack the myriad problems created by life in "a mass society."

Innovations in the electrical and chemical stimulation of the brain have brought physiological psychology much closer to a resolution of the structure-function dichotomy. The discovery of mediating centers in the subcortical regions promises a better understanding of neurophysiological mechanisms, and the cleavage between neurophysiology and psychology has definitely lessened. There is no likelihood today that psychology will some day be absorbed by a "break-through" in neurophysiology; even if the "internal environment" should be thoroughly mastered, there would still remain the problem of relating its functions to the "external environment."

The frontiers of scientific psychology are many and varied. Psychopharmacology, the study of the effect of drugs on behavior, has opened a new area of research; factor analytic studies of productive or creative thinking have suggested new methods of assessing intellectual abilities; engineering and mathematical principles imply more effective methods of studying human capacities; and the introduction of high-speed data-processing equipment has renewed concern with the psychological processes of problem-solving and decision-making.

But all is not optimism within the vast area encompassed by contemporary psychology. As we have seen, the demand for professional services has grown prodigiously since World War II, and the number of psychologists now engaged in professional pursuits exceeds the number who still identify themselves with the academic-scientific tradition. There is an increasing specialization of psychological services, and the bulk of current psychological research is applied research as opposed to basic or fundamental research.

An increasing concern with the application of psychological principles to immediate, concrete, practical problems has both its advantages and disadvantages. Much of the applied research in hospitals, industrial organizations, governmental agencies, commercial concerns, and educational institutions extends man's knowledge of his own behavior and furthers his understanding of human nature. But too much of such research is concerned with the solution of problems peculiar to the institution or organization in which the psychologist is employed.

The danger of psychology's future is that it will remain neither a science nor a profession but through absorption in pressing problems of predicting and controlling human behavior become merely a technology. Psychology *can* study man's behavior and it *can* improve man's condition, but it should not become a tool for merely manipulating man.

Bibliographical Notes

Because the contents of this book are part of the public domain of psychology, no attempt has been made to cite references. For those interested, however, the sources used in writing the book are given below. Although the works cited are by no means exhaustive, they present a fairly representative picture of psychology and may be regarded as a list of reading recommended for further study.

PHILOSOPHY OF SCIENCE

Several good treatments of the philosophy of science have appeared in recent years. H. Feigl and M. Brodbeck (eds.), *Readings in the Philosophy of Science* (Appleton-Century-Crofts, 1953); P. Frank, *Philosophy of Science: The Link Between Science and Philosophy* (Prentice-Hall, 1957); M. Marx, *Psychological Theory: Contemporary Readings* (Macmillan, 1963); and H. Reichenbach, *The Rise of Scientific Philosophy* (University of California Press, 1953) have influenced the author's thinking and may be recommended to those interested in the philosophical problems of psychology. An excellent treatment of the "philosophy" of research may be found in B. J. Underwood, *Psychological Research* (Appleton-Century-Crofts, 1957).

HISTORY AND SYSTEMS

The acknowledged classic in the history of psychology is E. G. Boring, *A History of Experimental Psychology* (Appleton-Century-Crofts, 1950). Equally interesting is E. G. Boring, *Sensation and Perception in the History of Psychology* (Appleton-Century-Crofts, 1942). A discussion of the historical development of psychology in terms of "its great men" may be found in R. I. Watson, *The Great Psychologists: Aristotle to Freud* (Lippincott, 1963). Systems and theories are covered unusually well by J. P. Chaplin and T. S.

Krawiec, *Systems and Theories of Psychology* (Holt, Rinehart and Winston, 1960); M. Marx and W. A. Hillix, *Systems and Theories in Psychology* (McGraw-Hill, 1963); and B. B. Wolman, *Contemporary Theories and Systems in Psychology* (Harper & Row, 1960). A superb treatment of the historical development of several selected research topics is given in Leo Postman (ed.), *Psychology in the Making* (Knopf, 1962).

INTRODUCTORY TEXTBOOKS

Textbooks used for introductory courses at the college level present a smorgasbord of principles, problems, theories, methods, and techniques. Psychology is presented in its many facets and the student is invited to take this choice; the development of "good eating habits" is left entirely to the discretion of instructors. Representative of introductory texts are: E. R. Hilgard, *Introduction to Psychology* (Harcourt, Brace & World, 1962); C. T. Morgan, *Introduction to Psychology* (McGraw-Hill, 1961); N. L. Munn, *Psychology* (Houghton Mifflin, 1961); F. L. Ruch, *Psychology and Life* (Scott, Foresman, 1963); and F. H. Sanford, *Psychology: A Scientific Study of Man* (Wadsworth, 1961).

Efforts to present a more systematic discussion have been made by R. M. Gagné and E. A. Fleishman, *Psychology and Human Performance* (Holt, Rinehart and Winston, 1959); F. Geldard, *Fundamentals of Psychology* (Wiley, 1962); D. M. Johnson, *Psychology: A Problem-Solving Approach* (Harper & Row, 1961); Howard Kendler, *Basic Psychology* (Appleton-Century-Crofts, 1963); D. J. Lewis, *Scientific Principles of Psychology* (Prentice-Hall, 1963); B. F. Skinner, *Science and Human Behavior* (Macmillan, 1953); and D. D. Wickens and D. R. Meyer, *Psychology* (Holt, Rinehart and Winston, 1961).

METHODS OF INQUIRY

Experimental methods are discussed in R. S. Woodworth and H. Schlosberg, *Experimental Psychology* (Holt, Rinehart and Winston, 1955); and C. E. Osgood, *Method and Theory in Experimental Psychology* (Oxford University Press, 1953). An excellent discussion of method, as opposed to content, is given in F. J. McGuigan, *Experimental Psychology: A Methodological Approach* (Prentice-Hall, 1960).

Statistical methods have been discussed in numerous textbooks. Those found most helpful by the author are: A. L. Edward, *Experimental Design in Psychological Research* (Holt, Rinehart and Winston, 1960); J. P. Guilford, *Fundamental Statistics in Psychology and Education* (McGraw-Hill, 1956); and J. P. Guilford, *Psychometric Methods* (McGraw-Hill, 1954).

Clinical methods as a method of inquiry are receiving increasing attention but no single book provides a comprehensive discussion. The author has relied heavily on H. B. Pepinsky and P. N. Pepinsky, *Counseling Theory and Practice* (Ronald, 1954); R. W. Wallen, *Clinical Psychology: The Study of Persons* (McGraw-Hill, 1956); and T. R. Sarbin *et al.*, *Clinical Inference and Cognitive Theory* (Holt, Rinehart and Winston, 1960).

TOPICS AND AREAS

The subject matter of psychology has been covered by a multitude of well-written textbooks, but only recently has a suitable interpretation for the general reader appeared. G. A. Miller, *Psychology: The Science of Mental Life* (Harper & Row, 1962) may be recommended to both the layman and the introductory student.

The following textbooks are not presented as a representative sample of textbooks in psychology. However, each book listed may be regarded as a competent treatment of the topic designated by its title:

Allport, F. H., *Theories of Perception and the Concept of Structure* (Wiley, 1955).

Anastasi, Anne, and J. P. Foley, *Differential Psychology* (Macmillan, 1949).

Cronbach, L. J., *Essentials of Psychological Testing* (Harper & Row, 1960).

Dember, W. N., *Psychology of Perception* (Holt, Rinehart and Winston, 1960).

Geldard, F. A., *The Human Senses* (Wiley, 1953).

Gilmer, B. V., *Industrial Psychology* (McGraw-Hill, 1961).

Goodenough, F., and L. Tyler, *Developmental Psychology* (Appleton-Century-Crofts, 1959).

Hahn, M. E., and M. S. MacLean, *Counseling Psychology* (McGraw-Hill, 1955).

Hall, C. S., and G. Lindzey, *Theories of Personality* (Wiley, 1957).

Hilgard, E. R., *Theories of Learning* (Appleton-Century-Crofts, 1956).

McCormick, E. J., *Human Engineering* (McGraw-Hill, 1957).

Morgan, C. T., and E. Stellar, *Physiological Psychology* (McGraw-Hill, 1950).

Pressey, S. L., F. P. Robinson, and J. E. Horrocks, *Psychology in Education* (Harper & Row, 1959).

Waters, R. H., D. A. Rethlingshafer, and W. E. Caldwell, *Principles of Comparative Psychology* (McGraw-Hill, 1960).

Webb, W. B., *The Profession of Psychology* (Holt, Rinehart and Winston, 1962).

Woodworth, R. S., *Dynamics of Behavior* (Holt, Rinehart and Winston, 1958).

Index

Probability, defined, 73; types of, 73–74
Professional psychology, 104–106; development of, 97–98
Progress, in science, 8
Projective techniques, 90–91
Pseudosciences of behavior, 5–6
Psychiatrists, distinguished from psychologists, 106
Psychoanalysis, 36–39, 40–41; psychoanalysts, 106
Psychological concepts, 45–48
Psychological determinism, 37, 43–44
Psychological laws, 44–45
Psychological testing, 29, 70–71, 82, 89–90, 93, 97
Psychological theory, 48–53
Psychology, as a science, 18
Psychopharmacology, 109
Psychophysics, 24–26, 70–71, 100

Quetelet, L. A., 70

Randomization, 63–64
Reinforcement, 46, 49

Sampling error, 67, 72–73
Science, problems in defining, 8–9
Scientific laws, 14; definition of, 15
Significant event, in psychology, 37, 39, 42
Situational variables, control of, 64–65; defined, 61
Social psychology, 103
Specific energies, doctrine of, 22
Spurzheim, J. G., 23–24

Statistical analysis of experimental results, 67–69, 78–79
Statistical methods, 53–55; and experimentation, 80–82, 108–109
Statistical psychology, 101–103
Structuralism, 29–31, 32, 33, 34, 36, 37–39, 40–41
Structure-function issue, 24, 30, 42, 109
Subject variables, control of, 62–64; defined, 61

Task variables, control of, 66; defined, 61–62
Technology, and science, 14, 109–110
Thales, 13
Theoretical constructs, 46–48
Theory in science, 17
Theory versus facts, 53
Thinking, 100
Thorndike, Edward L., 29
Titchener, Edward Bradford, 29–31
Treatment variables, control of, 65–66; defined, 61

Unconscious motivation, 36, 51

Verification in science, 17
Vesalius, 22
Vocational psychology, 102

Watson, John B., 33–34, 40
Weber, Ernst, 24–25
Weber-Fechner law, 25
Wertheimer, Max, 35
Wundt, Wilhelm, 26–27, 28